What Your Colleagues Are Saying . . .

Every educator and policy maker has ideas and knows exactly what will improve their school. That's the easy part. But does the solution really fit the need of the school? Do the school players have the commitment or readiness to venture forward? To get it right the first time, apply Marshall's model of implementation in your school.

—John Hattie
Emeritus Laureate Professor, University of Melbourne and
Co-director of the Hattie Family Foundation
Carlton, Victoria, Australia

This is the strongest and most comprehensive book I have read on the topic of implementation. James Marshall has a deep understanding of how school leaders and teachers need to implement initiatives, and he lays out how to do just that.

—Peter DeWitt
Corwin Author
Albany, New York

Right From the Start offers poignant examples, tools, and processes, and it inspires confidence in the potential for program and organizational transformation in multiple contexts. If you are seeking powerful, practical advice, this is the resource you've been looking for.

—Michelle D. Young
Dean, Loyola Marymount University School of Education
Professor of Leadership and Policy
Los Angeles, California

James Marshall has a wise and dynamic approach to program design. I wish I had found this book years ago.

—Virginia E. Kelsen
Assistant Superintendent, Glendora Unified School District
Claremont, California

James Marshall's practical guide offers schools an invalu_____ _____ ___
strategize efforts that will ensure the expected student ou_____ ____
read for leaders who are passionate about equity and excel____

—J_
Executive Director/National Center of Urban
Bonita, California

Every leader who strives to make a difference can benefit from James Marshall's practical guide with its clear language and powerful examples. I wish I had studied this book 40 years ago!

—Joseph F. Johnson
Founding Director, National Center for Urban School Transformation
Professor and Dean Emeritus, San Diego State University
San Diego, California

Right From the Start provides leadership teams with a simple yet detailed framework they can utilize to examine the suitability of a program and to develop suitable programs for their context. It will help you identify key elements for consideration to ensure a higher level of implementation success.

—**Ray Boyd**
West Swan (Dayton) Primary School
Brabham, Western Australia

These tools support planning, selecting, monitoring, evaluating, and revising your programs collaboratively to raise teacher and student performance. The intentional practices and questions lead from knowledge to action to reflection, with appreciative inquiry.

—Helene Alalouf
Educational Consultant
New York, New York

James Marshall provides guideposts to avoid common mistakes. You will find common sense approaches to building good programs—understand the audience, the needs, and the design with impact in mind. Stick with Marshall's wise observations and guidance to get it right for the long term.

—Debra Tica Sanchez
Senior Vice President, Educational Media and Learning Experiences
Corporation for Public Broadcasting
Washington, DC

This is an essential guide for moving ideas into practice. All too often we are disappointed when the intended outcomes of our initiatives are not achieved. Marshall's work provides what leaders need for action and success.

—**Andi Fourlis**
Superintendent, Mesa Public Schools
Mesa, Arizona

Right

FROM THE

START

Right
FROM THE
START

The ESSENTIAL GUIDE to
Implementing School Initiatives

JAMES MARSHALL
Foreword by Douglas Fisher

FOR INFORMATION:

Corwin

A SAGE Company

2455 Teller Road

Thousand Oaks, California 91320

(800) 233-9936

www.corwin.com

SAGE Publications Ltd.

1 Oliver's Yard

55 City Road

London EC1Y 1SP

United Kingdom

SAGE Publications India Pvt. Ltd.

Unit No 323-333, Third Floor, F-Block

International Trade Tower Nehru Place

New Delhi 110 019

India

SAGE Publications Asia-Pacific Pte. Ltd.

18 Cross Street #10-10/11/12

China Square Central

Singapore 048423

President: Mike Soules

Vice President and
   Editorial Director: Monica Eckman

Senior Acquisitions Editor: Tanya Ghans

Content Development
   Manager: Desirée A. Bartlett

Senior Editorial Assistant: Nyle De Leon

Project Editor: Amy Schroller

Copy Editor: Karin Rathert

Typesetter: C&M Digitals (P) Ltd.

Proofreader: Dennis Webb

Cover Designer: Gail Buschman

Marketing Manager: Morgan Fox

Printed in Canada

Library of Congress Control Number: 2023935919

This book is printed on acid-free paper.

MIX
Paper from
responsible sources
FSC® C103567

23 24 25 26 27 10 9 8 7 6 5 4 3 2 1

DISCLAIMER: This book may direct you to access third-party content via Web links, QR codes, or other scannable technologies, which are provided for your reference by the author(s). Corwin makes no guarantee that such third-party content will be available for your use and encourages you to review the terms and conditions of such third-party content. Corwin takes no responsibility and assumes no liability for your use of any third-party content, nor does Corwin approve, sponsor, endorse, verify, or certify such third-party content.

ASSESS
STRENGTHS
& NEEDS

EVALUATE
INITIATIVE

DESIGN
INITIATIVE

IMPLEMENT
INITIATIVE

Predictable Results

Strengths & Needs

DATA

Contents

PART II. DESIGNING AND LAUNCHING THE INITIATIVE 69

PART III. FROM IMPLEMENTATION TO IMPACT 137

List of Figures

List of Tables

Foreword

by Douglas Fisher

If there ever was a time that educators were inundated with initiatives, it is now. There are so many efforts, often funded by governments, designed to meet particular needs of specific students. Each of these initiatives has the *potential* to do some good, and we're thankful for the resources. But developing plans, coordinating the various efforts, not duplicating work already done (or in the official language of programs, supplementing and not supplanting), and monitoring the implementation can be overwhelming. In fact, some have argued that we exist in a perpetual state of *plan-maggedon,* in which we spend more time on the development of new plans for new initiatives and not enough time on implementation and monitoring impact. As a result, many of the initiatives that have great potential are a flop.

Fullan (2007) has taught us that change occurs over time and likely occurs in overlapping phases, from initiation to implementation to institutionalization. For an initiative to take hold, each of these phases is important and requires different actions.

The problem is that too much time is spent on initiation and not enough on implementation and institutionalization. In fact, upwards of 80% of the initiative efforts are devoted to initiation. It's not that initiation is unimportant. There are critical actions that must be taken at the start of an initiative. Unfortunately, many initiatives are left on the drawing board, so to speak. The plans have been initiated, perhaps the funding is secured, and the team is on to the next new thing. What gets left behind is the hard work of implementation and eventually, if the evidence supports it, going to scale with the ideas.

One of the challenges with initiation is what we decide to initiate. As Hattie (2009) notes, nearly everything we do in education "works" because it has a positive effect on students. But how much of an effect should our initiatives have? A minor positive effect is not likely worth the investment of time and resources. Interestingly, a child simply living for a year with no schooling achieves an effect size of 0.15. As Hattie notes, "Maturation alone can account for much of the enhancement of learning" (p. 16). Surely, we can do better than that.

Now, assuming we have a solid idea for an initiative or at least a way of responding to the funding opportunity that does no harm, then the hard work begins. There are so many distractions in education; we're continually searching for the proverbial silver bullet that will transform schools and their learners. Staying focused on the evidence-based ideas from the initiation phase is hard enough but is complicated by the fact that implementation is messy and fraught with conflict. As Mark Twain is purported to say, *"The only person who likes change is a baby with a wet diaper."* But the reality is that change is here to stay, and we need to figure out ways to support our colleagues in the change process.

When it comes down to it, we need tools to move from ideation to implementation. And we need tools to maintain our efforts and scale them, which is why *Right From the Start* came at just the right time for me. At our school, as I write, we're about to launch a community schools initiative. It's a fairly complex initiative, with four pillars (cpisandiego .org/community-schools):

- **Integrated student supports** that address out-of-school barriers through the coordination of trauma-informed health, mental health, and social services

- **Expanded and enriched learning time and opportunities** that include academic support, enrichment, and real-world learning opportunities (e.g., internships, project-based learning)

- **Family and community engagement**, which involves actively tapping the expertise and knowledge of family and community members to serve as true partners in supporting and educating students

- **Collaborative leadership and practices** for educators and administrators that establish a culture of professional learning, collective trust, and shared responsibility for outcomes in a manner that includes students, families, and community members

Even if this is not the initiative that you're involved with, you can see that it's complicated and complex. Our team has many ideas based on our needs assessment and developed an amazing proposal that was funded. Then the reality hit and we had to begin implementation. The tools in *Right From the Start* guided us in moving from the planning and initiation stage to the implementation stage. Although we are not yet at the stage of institutionalization, this book set the stage for us in terms of monitoring and making decisions. Yes, we have had to modify our course based on the evidence we have collected. And we are better because of it. And we are witnessing positive outcomes for students and staff as a result of actual implementation of the ideas.

Regardless of the particular initiative you're interested in, from changing a classroom practice to altering the ways that schools operate, don't fall in the trap of focusing exclusively on initiation. The students and staff in our schools deserve much more. And the tools to deliver on that promise are in your hands right now.

Acknowledgments

Writing a book is an intensely reflective task. While I've authored the pages you're about to read, that would have never happened without the many lived experiences and collaborations I've been so fortunate to have. Before we go any further, let me offer up credit where credit is due.

Here's to five mentors, thought partners, and provocateurs who have each influenced my thinking about initiatives in infinite ways. To Debra Erickson, for relentless encouragement that led me into this field and the pursuit of programs and their evaluation. To Allison Rossett, as professor and then colleague, for her unique and sense-making tactics in assessing performance and finding form and function through systems. To Margy Hillman, for her creative approaches to designing programs and our later escapades on scores of projects across scores of districts that have taught me much about initiative successes . . . along with what to avoid. To Bernice Stafford, for her unusually pragmatic insights into program implementation, evaluation, and impact . . . and for sharing her talents in making data sensible, actionable, and persuasive—all of which influence my work each and every day. And, finally, to Peggy O'Brien, perhaps my favorite collaborator and co-conspirator, who provided countless opportunities to pursue the ideas in this book, learn from our successes and yet-to-be successes, and simply have a ball each step of the way. Each of these smart, sagacious individuals lives in the pages of this book. I consider myself fortunate for having not only crossed paths, but for also having been invited to travel so many interesting roads together.

Here's to the countless educators, leaders, and generally brilliant people with whom I've worked. They've provided a set of wildly diverse experiences with educational initiatives—some planned, many unexpected. Top of mind, I share my gratitude for the smarts shared by Grace Ko and Laurie Mosier; Chantel Jimenez, Danielle Ross-Winslow, and Natalie Sexton; Edward Price, Charles De Leone, Debbie DeRoma, and

April Nelson; Michael Fragale, Fiona Macintyre, Sarah Bean, and Debra Tica Sanchez; Joaquin Ortiz; Leah Clapman; Rachel Miller and Jennifer Coronel; Laura Hunter; Victoria Garrison; Malaika Washington, Valerie Sims, Leah Robin, and Michelle Carman-McClanahan. I would immediately add to that the countless smart and innovative graduate students who influence my thinking while providing opportunities that challenge it too. And, finally, to Nick Stone and Sallie Saltzman for punctuating the pages with the helpful visuals you'll encounter, all in the spirit of bringing ideas to light.

Here's to amazing colleagues that lead by example, support unconditionally, and forever encourage the "what is," over the "what isn't." To Doug Fisher who issued the challenge for this book a few years back and never doubted that it would happen. My appreciation for your gentle encouragement and belief in the outcome cannot be overstated. To Nancy Frey for her always at-the-ready, just-in-time support that included countless answers to my novice "how to write a book" questions. Your generosity and input are appreciated more than you may know. To Diane Lapp for her endless encouragement, early reviews of the content, and general accountability that brought this book to fruition so that those beyond our students could benefit. To Marcie Bober, for our early and shared pursuits understanding, applying, and optimizing our teaching of program and product evaluation that persist in these pages. And to Peter Wayson, without whose guidance and critical reflection I don't think I would have made it past "go" following graduate school.

Here's to the latest and the most influential voice that significantly influenced the pages you're about to read—my senior editor Tanya Ghans. I've learned much from you throughout this process, while having quite a bit of fun along the way. I've never encountered anyone who is such a perfect a mix of helpfully critical, wonderfully collaborative, and clairvoyantly creative. This work is measurably better because of your contributions.

And here's to friends and family for being there and egging me on along the way. Those who know me would be quick to share that the last thing I would ever do is talk about the fact I was writing a book. Yet once that cat flew out of the bag, their support made all the difference. So thank you to the Kitchen Cabinet for your friendship and support, especially as I tried many of these ideas out with our own unique and shared "initiative"; my gratitude to the owners of the Lilikoi Lounge, which provides the best writing retreats an author could imagine—including requisite opportunities to achieve the perfect work-play balance; and my enduring appreciation to the proprietors of the Rumpus Room, who provided critical and requisite opportunities to relax, recharge, and reflect on life experiences included herein. Each of you has shaped and inspired the words on the pages that follow. For each of you, I am thankful.

Finally, to Eric, along with Wexler, Zoya, Gus, Xander, and Charley—my support team and the greatest source of motivation these many years. There isn't me today without the indelible influences you have each had on my life.

Publisher's Acknowledgments

Corwin gratefully acknowledges the contributions of the following reviewers:

Helene Alalouf
Educational Consultant
New York, NY

Ray Boyd
West Swan (Dayton) Primary School
Brabham, WA

Virginia E. Kelsen
Assistant Superintendent, Glendora Unified School District
Claremont, CA

About the Author

James Marshall's life-long work lies at the intersection of people and the organizations in which they work—and optimizing the synergy that fertile convergence holds. His scholarship, teaching, and consulting combine our understanding of human performance and organization development to assess strengths, devise strategy, and improve even the most vexing of challenges. Engagements have found him doing everything from evaluating virtual reality-delivered training for active shooter containment, to devising strategy that improved the community-focused impacts realized by the national network of over 150 public television stations.

He is currently Professor of Educational Leadership at San Diego State University, in the #1 ranked California State University College of Education. In his private practice, he serves as a thought partner to leaders seeking to hasten the collective impact of their organization's investments—especially their human resources. From assessing strengths and needs to conceptualizing strategy and initiatives and then measuring return on investment, Dr. Marshall's unique approach relies on a proven mix of assessment and evaluation, appreciative inquiry, and empathic understanding that predictably yields quantifiable results. Clients particularly note his ability to use data—with novelty and persuasion—to drive change.

With over 200 publications to his credit, Dr. Marshall's scholarship encompasses a diverse range of works that includes empirical research, program evaluation efforts, and policy development. His program evaluation endeavors are particularly significant and include over 250 individual studies of funded projects and program investments totaling more than $120 million dollars. This work has been funded by diverse agencies that include the National Science Foundation, the National Endowment for the Humanities, the Institute for Library and Museum Services, the Public Broadcasting Service, and the Corporation for Public Broadcasting, as well as the U.S. Department of Education, U.S. Department of Health and Human Services, U.S. Department of the Interior, and the Transportation Security Administration. His work with state and local education agencies, school systems, and regional offices of education encompasses forty of the fifty United States.

Internationally, Dr. Marshall has influenced human and organization performance through his service on the International Board of Standards for Training, Performance, and Instruction (IBSTPI) board of directors. Here, his needs assessment-focused research assisted the organization in better understanding its audiences and their needs, as IBSTPI reformulated its long-term strategy and support of learning leaders worldwide.

He can be reached at marshall@sdsu.edu.

Introduction

If Any Outcome
Will Do . . .

At the turn of the century, a consortium of school districts received funding to increase the abilities of teachers to teach history. Millions of dollars would support a multiyear, multicomponent program to both enhance teacher knowledge and change their "doing" as they applied that new content knowledge to teach their students. This setup is a familiar one. It's what I call the one-two punch: (1) enhance the teacher's content and pedagogical repertoire and then (2) successfully apply it in the classroom. Thereafter, student learning and achievement follows. As learning leaders, we know learning is not enough in the absence of application—whether applied to our teaching staff or our students.

Partnering in this endeavor would be esteemed history professors from a local, prestigious university. The program director worked with the university's history department chair to shape the professional development the teachers would experience. When it came to evaluating the program, which was the role I played, this was a dream project. That's because I was part of it from the beginning. I authored a tentative evaluation plan, matched to the high-level envisioned design, which was all part of the grant proposal.

With funding in hand, planning discussions continued, and as the program components were plotted on a timeline, I became curious. Acknowledging what is perhaps limitless possibilities in the annals of history, I queried the university partner as to the scope and ideally focus of the history content for this project. Their response to me was candid and went something like this: "You know, I wish I could tell you. But my assumption is that each faculty member will just reach into their desk ten to fifteen minutes before their scheduled teacher presentation, sift through some transparencies, select a few, and come and speak for the allotted time." To fully appreciate the picture in your mind, transparencies predated PowerPoint and were acetate pages used on an overhead projector. That said, this was mid-2000, PowerPoint was well established, and the transparencies, I believe, signaled the recency of the content . . . perhaps not in a positive way.

As someone who considers himself an intentional planner, I was stunned (while, of course, keeping a poker face). I left worried. Had I just witnessed a textbook case of this important initiative's early veering off its track? By the way—if you're picturing this situation, you've probably noticed that what happened here is basically acknowledging there is no, nor will there be any, "track." Stunning.

As I walked to my car that day, here is the beginning of the list of the worries that swirled in my mind:

- Will the spontaneous and serendipitous presentation of history content simply duplicate the existing knowledge of the participating teachers?
- Will the presented history content align with state standards that drive the participating teachers' instruction?
- Will the presented history topics be of interest to our participating teachers?
- Will the presented history content be areas in which the participating teachers struggle and where they could "up their game?"
- And across our participating group of teachers, will their diverse needs each be met—including preparing each to apply the content equitably with their equally diverse students?

You probably noticed that the first four things on this list are *participant* focused. It shouldn't be a surprise. If we truly want these kinds of initiatives to change lives, they must meet our participants where they are while also meeting their recognized needs. And yet, when faced with a new and novel opportunity, it is easy for leaders to lose track of that priority. These able and willing U.S. History teacher participants were about to "get what they get" rather than get something relevant and aligned to their world and their students' needs.

While there are multiple lessons to learn from this scenario, it offers a vivid non-example of focusing on the program's history teacher participants. The good news is that, over time, the teams met in the middle—as a result of program evaluation findings and a commitment to continuous improvement over the grant period. In the end, together we achieved something that was both relevant and aligned . . . but the original timeline was tripled.

So what's wrong with throwing caution to the wind and letting serendipity rule the day? Well first, most initiatives involving change come at a cost. Many require a school system's investment. The cost of pursuing one initiative includes not providing access to any number of other, possibly needed, efforts in your school. Additionally, most funded programs involve accountability to the local, state, or federal government who made the investment. But aside from each of these compelling reasons, failing to focus the outcomes and then align everything the initiative involves to those outcomes leaves students vulnerable.

What This Book Will Do for You

This book is all about initiatives—those in your school or across your district, those you present in partnership with people and organizations in your community, and those funded by the state and federal government. And most importantly, it is about turning your ideas into living, thriving, and impact-making initiatives.

Initiatives? Aren't We Really Talking About Programs Here?

If I was writing this book ten years ago, you would have just read something like, "This book is all about programs." But I believe our contemporary work as leaders must go beyond the traditional definition of "program." Many of the things we'll talk about are, in a historical sense, "programs." But here is a not-so-little secret: Programs dropped into schools and districts often fail—not always because they're not good . . . but rather because we fail to respect the true, change-inducing designs they involve and the implementations they demand.

Think about a textbook adoption. It's just about picking a book and buying it in quantity, right? If only it were that simple. The adoption of a new resource—or, shall I say, the *successful* adoption of a new resource—immediately rises to the "initiative" level. From the selection and purchase to training for classroom educators, developing wraparound supports, establishing expectations for implementation, and continuously monitoring this change process for purposes of both continuous improvement and confirmation of impact . . . to be successful, it must be recognized as the initiative it presents. Look at all that's to be done, nicely simplified into just one sentence! As leaders, you can quickly envision what such a process might require along with the time it would take to do it right.

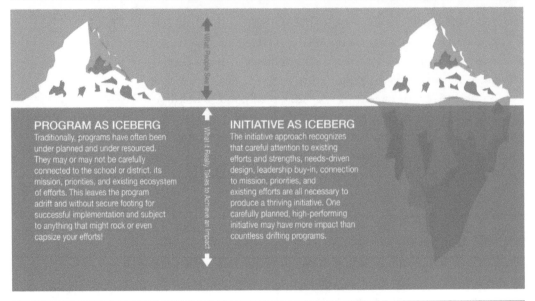

Figure I.1   Iceberg Model Comparison of Programs and Initiatives

PROGRAM AS ICEBERG
Traditionally, programs have often been under planned and under resourced. They may or may not be carefully connected to the school or district, its mission, priorities, and existing ecosystem of efforts. This leaves the program adrift and without secure footing for successful implementation and subject to anything that might rock or even capsize your efforts!

INITIATIVE AS ICEBERG
The initiative approach recognizes that careful attention to existing efforts and strengths, needs-driven design, leadership buy-in, connection to mission, priorities, and existing efforts are all necessary to produce a thriving initiative. One carefully planned, high-performing initiative may have more impact than countless drifting programs.

How to Use This Guide

I've authored the book to build, confirm, and extend your knowledge about initiative planning, implementation, and evaluation. It is separated into three parts: **Getting Smart Through Needs Assessment (Part I)**, **Designing and Launching the Initiative (Part II),** and **From Implementation to Impact (Part III)**. It also includes the following:

- Tools for analysis and documentation
- Self-assessments
- Real-world examples (Tales From the Field)
- Discussion questions
- Pacing suggestions
- Glossary (terms in the glossary will appear in **bold** the first time they are defined in the text)

While you'll encounter the individual tools throughout the book, I've provided the full toolset for your use in Appendix C.

How you move forward with the book will depend on who you are, where you're working, what kinds of challenges you're facing, and how much time you can invest. While the book is written in a story-like fashion that you can read cover to cover, it's also organized so that you can quickly drop in on any stage of the initiative lifecycle at your time of need. Here are some other ideas of how different people in a variety of roles might use the comprehensive guidance and tools I've included.

- **Principals** can use this book to consider, craft, and create initiatives at the school level where they might use less formal initiative and evaluation plan documentation as they fold initiative work into their daily effort.

- **District leaders** can use this book to posit, plan, and pursue initiatives of all kinds, sizes, and complexities as they moderate the amounts of needs assessment, initiative documentation, and evaluation to the expectations of their team members and overseers.

- **Instructional coaches** can use this book to assess needs, design performance-focused initiatives, and measure their impact as part of their commitment to continuous improvement.

- **Teachers** can use this book as they design classroom-scale, grade-level, or discipline-wide initiatives that are responsive to student strengths and needs while directly contributing to learning and doing.

- **Everyone else** can benefit from this book by following the systematic design process you'll learn, which lends form to the entire effort, all the while keeping us focused on the people that will be involved in the initiative (participants and supporters) and the intended outcomes.

I'll assert that most of what I'll share is applied common sense. Yet because of our fast-paced lives and the endless press to get things done, we often forgot to reflect and apply that common sense to our benefit. But here is the promise I make: If you spend the necessary time to develop a something that is responsive to demonstrated needs, carefully reflects the participants involved, and integrates formative and summative evaluation to continuously improve results, your implementation will avoid the common pitfalls that send otherwise reasonable initiatives to the "didn't work for us" bin.

Setting the Stage

What Is an Initiative?

Throughout this guide, I will interchange the terms *program* and *initiative* because of how strongly their meanings overlap. However, there is a bit of daylight between them, and I will address that now.

I've suggested that successful programs reside within larger, carefully planned initiatives. Let's first define program. *Merriam-Webster* indicates that a program is "a plan or system under which action may be taken toward a goal." Breaking that down, for something to be a program, it needs

- a plan or defined system that guides action, and
- the action must be aligned with and move us closer toward a defined goal.

Next, let's consider the definition of initiative. This time, consulting the *Oxford English Dictionary*, we find that an initiative—and I really like this—is "an act or strategy intended to resolve a difficulty or improve a situation; a fresh approach to something." As leaders, doesn't that resonate perfectly with what we seek to do?

Defining Initiatives

One thing is certain: No matter who we are, we are surrounded by initiatives each day. So far this morning, I participated in a virtual, online cycling exercise program; prepared a presentation to share a new Teacher-Leader master's program we're offering at San Diego State University with potential participants; checked in with the district manager of a Centers for Disease Control and Prevention (CDC) Sexual Health Education funded program that I evaluate for a large, urban school district; and reported how I'm feeling following a COVID vaccine to the v-check program. And it's only 10:00 a.m.

Now, think about the spaces where we work. As educational leaders, we are surrounded by learning initiatives. They're already familiar. A new mathematics curriculum, a social-emotional learning initiative across the district, a professional development effort around evidence-based strategies—each can be considered an initiative. Recognize that the initiatives we pursue in our schools almost always target some change in knowledge. But they also should target some change in behavior . . . in what we do. That means knowing isn't enough. Targeting knowing alone will fall short of impact. And that is a problem because impact is the change we almost always want.

My work creating and evaluating education initiatives for over thirty years suggests something about education leaders: You *love* creating impactful learning experiences. Why wouldn't you? You pursued this profession to help all kinds of people learn, to creatively craft experiences that make that happen, and ultimately, to change lives.

Doing, however, isn't as commonly considered. Think about it: As a result of learning, what do we want to happen? Perhaps more importantly, how do we "bake" doing into the programs we design to ensure predictable "doing" happens for everyone who engages? Not to worry, we'll get there!

Slowing Your Roll

This multi-part guide for planning, implementing, and evaluating *learning-and-doing* initiatives comes with some important asks, from me to you. Let me take a moment to put them on the table.

First, I'm going to ask you to stop thinking about all the great things your initiative might include. I'm going to ask you to hold off on drawing conclusions about what you need . . . just for a bit. And perhaps the most difficult: I'm going to ask you to not worry about how you'll pay or not pay for whatever it is you've got in mind during the first phase of the work.

What I am going to ask you to do now is reflect on what brought you to the point of even thinking about some new initiative.

- Your students' literacy scores have been steadily declining for the past four years.
- Your teachers should know more about reflective practice.
- The superintendent just came back from a conference and saw an amazing new *Arts in Action* program they are keen on starting back home.
- There's an exciting new grant program from the U.S. Department of Education that could provide more than $3 million over the next three years to help you improve new teacher retention.

Each of these poses a potentially great opportunity. In fact, I'll admit to getting just a little excited just thinking about each of them. Maybe you, too, find yourself saying, "Yes! We *should* have an amazing arts program!" Or, "Our teachers would *love* learning more about reflective practice." Yet your response should really be, "Our teachers *might love* learning more about reflective practice . . . let's ask them and take some time to figure that out and what that would look like here in our district." Another good response, "Our teachers *might love* learning more about reflective practice . . . I'm excited to hear from them about this so we can tailor a program that will match their needs." You see, *you* are not one of the teachers who would be involved. Regrettably, you are probably also not clairvoyant. If you are to craft a successful program for someone who is not yourself, begin by taking a giant step back.

There are times I've felt like a "dream killer" when such words and phrases spring forth from my mouth, as I coach school leaders or sit at the table in the program evaluator role. Yet having seen too many programs miss the mark, sometimes because they fail to even establish a mark, I'm compelled to be the voice of reason at the earliest of stages. I know that some careful, intentional front-end needs assessment will yield predictable results in the long run, when "initiative meets world."

First Get Smart(er); Then Get Planning

Therefore, a good chunk of this first section is about understanding the place where initiatives happen, typically the school environment, and the people who must engage. I'm going to challenge you to take the time to understand both what *isn't* and what *is*. In the end, I predict you will enjoy taking this initial step back, engaging with your staff, and doing something good listening. To be fully successful, you'll have to suspend assumptions and do your absolute best to look at things with **fresh eyes**—setting aside your current understanding, presumptions, and biases and attempting to look at the situation anew. Remember, the dictionary definition of "initiative" included "a fresh approach to something." If you're currently leading a school, you might have a deep understanding about the people, needs, and programs that surround you. Set them aside, for now, and proceed with a mindset dedicated to both discovery and wonder. I promise, it will be worth the effort.

Where to Begin?

One thing I love about the initiatives is how they shape the people our students become tomorrow. Think back to some of the programs that got your attention and engagement when you were growing up—how some shaped who you did and did not become.

Can you remember a time when, during a training or professional development session that was content rich, you found yourself saying, "they really get me" or "it's like they knew exactly what I needed"? Well, "they" is the person who did the designing. And the process of "getting you" happened in one of two ways: either (1) dumb luck—which is unlikely—or (2) careful investigation of your needs and what's required to get you from where you are to where you need to be. Here is also where I'll suggest a program effectively rises to become an initiative—because it goes beyond some "event" to truly promote and sustain positive change over time.

Now, you may also recall times when a program completely missed the mark. Symptoms here include experiences you deemed a waste of time, irrelevant, compulsory, or just plain ineffective. Oh—one more symptom I'm sure you'll appreciate: a program you completed but never once used—save perhaps a completion certificate that now serves as wallpaper.

Hitting the Mark

I used the term "hit the mark" earlier as a rather quick way of describing initiatives that carefully target learning-and-doing outcomes and that predictably see each participant reaching those targets. At the risk of belaboring my point, hitting the mark doesn't happen by chance. Rather, it involves a hearty mix of inquiry, target setting, implementation planning, and adjustment.

Perhaps most important is the simple fact that hitting the mark isn't going to happen where

- there is no mark,

- there are too many marks,

- the mark is ambiguous, or

- everyone is picturing different marks or interpreting a "defined mark" in different ways.

As a school leader, how can you design initiatives that not only hit the mark but do so predictively for all participants? The process begins with a careful review of the current situation. We work to understand needs and the people involved and then craft a mix of solutions which, when combined, comprise an implementable program. It's no coincidence that Abraham Lincoln is credited, by some, as saying, "Give me six hours to chop down a tree and I will spend the first four sharpening the axe."

The initial axe sharpening work means **getting smart** about the following:

- Who is involved?

- What precipitated the new idea for this program?

- What is the current state of things?

- How does the current state differ from visions of the "ideal" state?

- What is happening currently that serves to keep your school where it is rather than where you'd like it to be?

The process of answering these questions is often referred to as needs assessment and it is key to initiative planning.

Needs Assessment: A Tool Naturally Aligned With Leadership

As a leader, you are responsible for helping people see context. You must interest and motivate them to come along. The **needs assessment** skills you are about to discover will benefit any leader—whether you're designing an initiative or simply trying to understand a challenging situation. I predict you will call upon the **human/organization performance categories** you'll soon learn in your daily practice. It will help you better understand the world and the people around you.

Setting the Stage Wrap-Up: Meet Linda

Before we get too far, I want to introduce you to a friend and educational leader. You see, we've faced challenging situations during our regular work with staff, students, parents, community members—you name it. We've also pressed through the process and guidance I'm about to share with you.

Linda is an amazing staff developer within one of our local elementary school districts. She's responsible for the professional development for more than forty elementary schools, all within the K–8 grade span. Linda doesn't consider her work professional development but instead refers to it as "professional learning." Linda's been doing this work for twenty years, and she absolutely loves helping teachers be the best they can be. And that's a really good thing—because her work is critical when you consider she is planning, coordinating, and presenting training (or learning) for more than 1,600 TK–5 teachers in her district. She's also new to this district—having just taken helm of the professional learning team within the last year.

Linda is facing the district-wide implementation of a new family engagement initiative next year. In fact, she's part of the team that is working to figure out the program right now.

We'll check in with her again the end of Parts I, II, and III, but I wanted to introduce you now because understanding her journey will help you apply many of the initiative elements I'll share.

Getting Smart Through Needs Assessment

What would you think, if upon walking into your doctor's office, she took one look at you and handed you a prescription? Unthinkable. And yet, when we launch into initiative design without taking time to understand the people involved, we are blindly prescribing without a proper diagnosis . . .

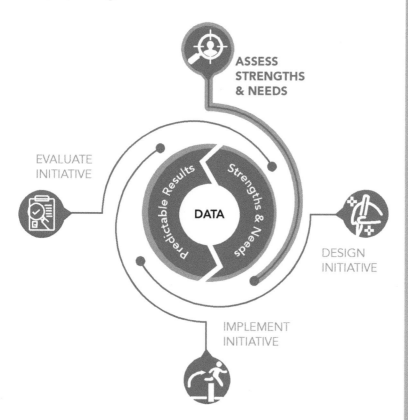

In Part I You Will . . .

- Analyze needs based on a defined, optimal outcome
- Categorize the types of strengths and barriers that drive success for people and the organizations in which they work and learn
- Get guidance on collecting data to inform your initiative design
- Review approaches to organizing data, as you draw conclusions that will influence your initiative's design

Key Tools

Tool 1: Realizing the 3Vs

Tool 2: Asking Good Questions

Tool 3: Data Collection Methods to Consider

Tool 4: Needs Assessment Headline Authoring Tool

Self-Assessment: Conducting Needs Assessment

Use this quick self-assessment to help you determine your prior knowledge for topics covered in Part I.

HOW MUCH DO YOU KNOW ABOUT . . .	A LOT	A LITTLE	NOT AT ALL	UNSURE
• How to assess needs	O	O	O	O
• Opportunity gaps	O	O	O	O
• Appreciative inquiry	O	O	O	O
• Performance drivers for successful initiatives	O	O	O	O
• When and how to gather quantitative and qualitative data	O	O	O	O
• The value of assessing needs	O	O	O	O

Success Starts With Understanding Needs 1

As a leader, you have undoubtedly encountered a chain of events that culminates in someone—a coach or consultant for example—sharing a "great idea for a program" or a "we should be doing this!" The simple fact that the current situation isn't how *they feel it should be* suggests the presence of a *gap*. Logic then follows that there are two related factors at play in this situation:

- The way things should be
- The way things currently are

Using basic and familiar deficit modeling, defining the gap is at first glance simple. Consider it like the subtraction problems you encountered in elementary school:

The Way Things Should Be

▬▬ The Way Things Currently Are

Gap

How do we know a gap when we see one? Let's look at some examples:

- Sixty percent of your students' test scores in reading are below standard, while all need to be at or above standard.
- Schools across your district should all have partnerships with local libraries, but only six out of twenty currently do.

- Teachers should be successfully implementing the new math curriculum in their classrooms, but observations indicate that only five have attempted to do so and only two are implementing based on the program guidelines.

- Students should understand and practice mindfulness techniques each day in class, yet very few can even name the five techniques we have covered.

Each of these examples defines what I consider the **primary gap.** Primary gaps are typically the result of multiple **contributing gaps.** Yet those proposing change often talk at the primary gap level; broad, sweeping strokes about a better reality through elimination of some perceived gap. Their words may sound basic, but we are often persuaded by their simple acknowledgement of a program need and the argument that something must be done. Yet this isn't the ideal place for you to start.

When confronted with such "gap evangelism," I suggest showing interest while planning for inquiry. This type of work almost always involves far more than simply addressing that top-level gap. The primary gap often offers the *call to action*. But designing a successful program will undoubtedly require a more *nuanced understanding of the contributing gaps that, together, define the entire situation—or system.* Yes, system. That's what you'll uncover as you examine all levels of gaps and come to understand how everything fits together to bring about the situation as currently presented. Forewarning: The system you'll uncover is usually messy; it is often political too.

Where We're Headed

Defined gaps, followed by an understanding of the barriers and strengths that allow those gaps to exist, inform the design or selection of programs that improve the gaps. This process is essentially making sure the square-pegged hole is filled with an equally square-pegged program.

When initiatives are predicated on solid data that reflect the voice, views, and visions of those involved, the chance of **predictable results** increases; **equitable results** too.

While the concept of gaps and the process of doing gap analysis may seem straightforward, success requires some unique skills and involves some specific steps I've begun to describe. Before you get too far and in the interest of offering a balanced perspective on program design and evaluation, let's contemplate a fact about **gap analysis** that few would bother bringing up.

Balancing the Deficit Focus Gaps Involve

In practice, you will find that the parlance used for gaps can vary. Here are some common ways people chat about them:

- Ideal state versus current state
- Wants versus haves
- Optimals versus actuals
- Oughts rather than ares

In the end, each pair represents the same type of equation and definition of the difference—and, let's admit, sometimes it's an intimidating chasm—between where we are now and where we need to be.

This routine is familiar because we have been encouraged to think in gaps most of our lives.

- To graduate, I must take each class on the provided program of study; thus far, I've completed twenty-two out of sixty.
- The job I want requires these qualifications, and I only meet half of those listed.
- I need $20,000 to buy a car, but my current savings is only $15,000.

What do these examples make you feel? If you're feeling less than enthused, there's good reason. They're all about what *isn't* and almost never involve what *is*.

Gap analysis is, by definition, a deficit approach. But that doesn't mean it can't and shouldn't be approached with some appreciative balance. Figure 1.1 uses a "crossing the river" analogy to demonstrate this important point. When all you see is the rushing river standing between where you are and where you need to be, you can become fixated on what you do not have. By widening your view and embracing all that surrounds that primary rushing river gap, you gain the bigger picture, which likely includes things that will support your effort to close the gap.

Figure 1.1   Balanced Approach to Gap Analysis

SEEING ONLY THE GAP:
DEFICIT FOCUS

TAKING TIME TO GET SMART:
GAPS AND STRENGTHS FOCUS

Appreciative Inquiry

Appreciative inquiry is a strengths-based approach based on the belief that deficit-based thinking stands to amplify problems in organizations rather than reduce them. Appreciative inquiry advocates look for the best in what currently is, while also defining the possible—what "could be"—in tangible terms.

Originally conceived by Cooperrider and Srivastva (1987), authors have more recently reflected upon the model and its use. In a comparison of appreciative inquiry to the more traditional approach to challenges, they suggested that traditional tactics treat organizations as *problems to be solved,* while appreciative inquiry approaches the organization as a *mystery to be embraced* (Cooperrider & Whitney, 2001). I ask you, who doesn't love a bit of mystery to keep things interesting?

With attention to the intersection between gap analysis and appreciative inquiry, our pursuits to understand a situation can go beyond deficits. Instead, the focus is to investigate gaps by looking for and seeking to understand areas where performance is falling short as well as areas of strength that can be leveraged in support of reaching the envisioned ideal. As I said earlier, this is the "things going right" approach.

It's important to acknowledge why people's knee-jerk reaction is to reject the positive. Maybe you've heard or even thought some of the following: "Focusing on what we're already doing isn't going to solve the problem." "Building on strengths is such a weak way to look at this, you've gotta focus on the problem to solve it." "Good luck with that warm and fuzzy thinking, it's not going to change anything." I could, can, and do counter each of these objections to a balanced approach—both to needs assessment and program evaluation. When my efforts involve a balanced approach that is dedicated to surfacing deficits alongside strengths and possibilities, I typically see improvements in the work, the trust, and the motivation of the project teams. It only makes sense when you consider, among other things, the hope that recognizing strengths provides—as opposed to stopping short once deficits are defined.

As leaders, I'd like you to consider this fact: When people shoot down the practice of embracing an appreciative balance to the work, it will tell you something about them, their organizational culture, or both. It might reflect their on-the-job existence is overly ruled by fixing gaps, with limited opportunity for strategy.

Here's another interesting thing about **countering objectives** to appreciative inquiry: While these criticisms are occasionally heard on the front end, I have *never* had anyone criticize the integration of strengths when I am presenting needs analysis results and initiative-related recommendations. In fact, pointing out strengths in the presence of barriers seems to put oxygen back into the room!

What's Going on Here?
Barriers and Strengths

2

With gaps defined, let's now focus on the "why." In this section, I will ask you to go deep to identify **root causes**. I sometimes think of it like a mystery to solve as I work to fully understand the likely many things that influence the gap.

Gap Influencers: Types of Barriers and Strengths

When you contemplate the things that influence a gap, let's first acknowledge that some of our influencing barriers and strengths rest within (think, intrinsic) the *people* involved, and some of the influencers are external forces that are under the control of the *organizations* in which we work and learn. **Behavioral engineering** (Gilbert, 2007) suggests that, as humans, there are things that drive and underlie everything we do and everything we don't do. Said another way, there are things that must be in place for us to complete any expectation with success. That includes the very things our initiatives seek to support people in achieving.

There are four categories of influencers. Table 2.1 and Figure 2.1 provide a quick overview of the categories and a description of where their influence originates.

The categories draw upon the work of three individuals. First, Gilbert (2007), who is considered by many to be the originator of human performance technology. Second, Mager and Pipe (1997), who leveraged Gilbert's work into a helpful framework for analyzing performance problems, defining goals and objectives, and measuring results. And third and most significantly, Rossett (2009), who streamlined these ideas into a set of conditions that are equally helpful and efficient. Rossett also offered the people/organization dichotomy, which helps organize thinking and the solutions upon which your initiatives will rely.

Table 2.1   Barriers and Strengths Category Overview

FOCUS	4 CATEGORIES OF BARRIERS/ STRENGTHS	SHORT DESCRIPTION
People	1. Skills and Knowledge	Possessing the necessary skill and knowledge to successfully perform
	2. Motivation	Having value for the work (they care and see why) and confidence in being successful (self-efficacy)
Organization	3. Incentives	Rewards of all kinds that come from performing
	4. Environment	Necessary tools and equipment; aligned policies and tactics—in sum, expectations and available time to perform

Figure 2.1   Barrier and Strength Categories

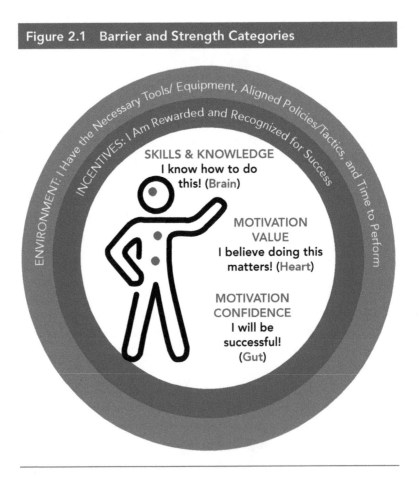

DID YOU KNOW? WHEN PEOPLE DON'T DO WHAT THEY SHOULD

When titling their book *Analyzing Performance Problems*, Mager and Pipe (1997) chose the subtitle, "They Really Outta Wanna." Isn't it the truth?

- Teachers aren't implementing the new and innovative instructional practices we spent three weeks learning about over summer.

- Students just cannot seem to "get" the order of operations.

- Our annual test scores fell short of expectations, and our students should want to do better.

- That zero-waste, school recycling initiative has done nothing to reduce our carbon footprint!

If you're the one in charge of the school or in charge of the related initiative, it's so easy to find yourself saying, "They really outta wanna do this," and for so many reasons!

But the plain truth is that the "knowing" part is really only the tip of the iceberg when it comes to people being successful in meeting outcomes—no matter what they are. Years of collective work has helped to estimate the frequency with which different "barriers" forestall reaching the sort of "performance-based" outcomes our initiatives involve. Whether it's teachers applying professional development in their classrooms, new leaders finding success in building the master calendar, or students producing a play they wrote, having the "knowing how" is just one part of the larger system that governs doing—and especially successful doing.

While the existing research comes largely from the business and not school world, it's safe to suggest that what we have learned transfers to the training and performance of leaders and staff within school systems.

(Continued)

(Continued)

Over time, research has established that when something isn't happening, it's likely *not* the result of not knowing how. I like the way Stolovitch and Maurice (1998) say it:

> More than 80% of performance gaps have little to do with skill and knowledge deficiencies. Rather, they are mostly the result of

- Inadequate information (e.g., lack of clear expectations; insufficient and/or untimely feedback; incomplete documentation)

- Insufficient tools and resources (e.g., procedures, equipment, personnel)

- Inappropriate, inadequate, and even counterproductive incentives (e.g., lack of appropriate rewards for desired performance; punishments for doing the right thing; rewards for non-accomplishments)

- Task interferences that place obstacles in the path of achieving desired ends (p. 10)

OK. That language may sound a little stilted when read by a school leader. The point remains that our initiatives really need to heed this simple and poignant fact. When someone isn't doing what we want, it's all too common to assume they need some good PD. "Train em up," we simply conclude. Yet doing that—or doing only that—as our "fix" won't fix anything approximately 80% of the time (Dean, 1994; Gilbert, 2007; Rummler & Brache, 1996; Stolovitch & Keeps, 1992).

The People 3

The first two types of barriers and strengths are things that "reside" within each of the people involved in the gap you're assessing. You might say they are the **intrinsic drivers** that support people being successful—whether it's implementing a new teaching strategy or performing on a high stakes test.

Skills and Knowledge

Any successful performance is driven by an individual's knowledge and skill. Sometimes, gaps are simply the result of missing knowledge or the unpolished ability to perform a learned skill. Many—maybe even most—of the initiatives you'll select or design are often attending to this very performance condition. A new mathematics curriculum seeks to positively impact the knowledge and skill of our students. Or a successful professional development program is designed to evolve the knowledge of our teachers and equip them with practiced skills for implementing it with their students. Even a student performance gap is often attributed to the knowledge and skill barrier.

When a gap is the result of a knowledge or skill shortcoming, it may feel like coming home! As seasoned educator, you've pretty much dedicated your life to helping people acquire or perfect varied domains of human knowledge. When knowledge and skill is behind the gap we're seeing, it may be easy to think "Ah yes . . . gotcha! I know exactly how to handle this" and go about whipping up a great learning experience or opportunity for practice. The problem with that approach is this: Human performance is far more complex.

Early research in this area has found that less than 20% of identified gaps are solely the result of missing knowledge and skill. Yes, 20%! That means, if the solutions you consistently adopted or created to address primary gaps were ones solely designed to teach and train (i.e., address skills/knowledge barriers), 80% of the time you'd not fully close the identified gap (Dean, 1994; Gilbert, 2007; Rummler & Brache, 1996; Stolovitch & Keeps, 1992).

Programs designed to address knowledge and skill gaps suffer from being our knee jerk reaction anytime someone isn't doing what they are supposed to be doing. In such crises, cries to "get them some PD," echo the hallway. I'm not suggesting it can't help. There may well be a knowledge and skill element present—and perhaps even a significant one. But when we fail to consider that other things may also be influencing the problem, we immediately limit the success our efforts will have. I said early on we don't just want a program; we want an initiative. And we want an initiative that yields predictable and equitable results. Being comprehensive in our design is how we make that happen, and understanding the full range of influences tells us how comprehensive to be.

What if you find the people involved fully possess the knowledge and skill necessary to perform—to implement curriculum in the classroom, to complete performance tasks on the annual state test? Mager and Pipe (1997) coined the **life dependency test** for this kind of situation: Placed into a do or die situation, if their lives depended on it, could they evidence the knowledge or skill? Extreme? Yes. But it quickly positions the fundamental question here: Do they or don't they have the necessary knowledge and skills? And let's just take a moment to also admit there are many things people know and *can* do that are also things people *choose not* to do or are limited by external factors in fully doing.

When you find the necessary knowledge and skill or perhaps even some related knowledge and skill are present, document it as a strength. Remember, we have committed ourselves to finding influences that both negatively and positively, even potentially positively, influence our gaps. When it comes to designing an initiative, strengths provide the strongholds. They can serve as fertile ground into which we "root" our program implementation.

Motivation = Value × Confidence

Much of the time, when I don't do something, it is motivation that I lack. I often possess the necessary knowledge and skills to perform . . . but, well, things get in the way. When we hear someone say, "They're just not motivated," it's mostly a fuzzy way of saying, "They could do it if they wanted to . . . if they chose to," and they're often right . . . they could! But when we are examining gaps—both the deficit and appreciative—how do we know it is a "choose to" problem? The short answer is we have to be careful. Here's why: You may be too quick to ascribe lack of motivation when someone isn't performing the way you want, and this is too fuzzy. So let's make motivation a bit more concrete and actionable.

The Motivation Equation

Expectancy theory (Vroom, 1964) is what we need to investigate and understand the motivation of the people involved in our gap. This theory offers two elements that, when multiplied conceptually, estimate a person's motivation. Here's what the equation looks like:

$$value \times confidence = motivation$$

Value is the first element in this equation. It describes the level of importance the individual ascribes to a given performance. Remember, this is an *intrinsic* measure. It is fully determined by the person who does the valuing. Sure, there could be very good external incentives present (good grades, money, a better state of life). But it's up to me to decide how much, if at all, those external factors affect the level of value I hold.

It's also helpful to think of value as an indication of how much someone *cares* about doing something—be it learning, performing, or any other action. When a gap is present because value is low, you'll likely hear people saying things like "oh, no one cares about that" or "that's fine for someone else, but not me." Of course, where value is high, we want to capture that as a strength and leverage it in support of the program we'll eventually design. Again, catch things going right when they're present.

The other half of the motivation equation is **confidence.** Confidence describes a person's belief that they can be successful. It's our own intrinsic judgment about whether we will succeed or fail. Another term you've probably heard used is *self-efficacy*. Bandura (1995) defined self-efficacy as "the belief in one's capabilities to organize and execute the courses of action required to manage prospective situations" (p. 2). Self-efficacy or confidence matters mightily. Think of the daily choices you make, many without intentional thought, that are based on confidence. We naturally gravitate toward doing the familiar things that we know will bring us success. Trying something that is new or novel, especially something we perceive as challenging, usually means we must confront worries about not being successful. When a gap is caused by lack of confidence, the program we develop must attend to the deficit.

We've all started learning experiences where we immediately felt in over our head. If you picture yourself in such a situation, you can feel the way it threatens your self-efficacy. Often the fright or flight reflex kicks into gear. Thus, one common way to mediate such confidence-threatening situations is simply shutting down. That often means quitting, which is something you absolutely do not want your teachers to do! For that reason alone, it's critical for you to always be mindful about confidence. Hopefully, this is something already on the minds of leaders. I encourage you consider it within the "value x confidence" equation for a powerful way of assessing motivation.

Putting value and confidence together offers some interesting "blends" that can be used in broad strokes to describe the people your program will involve. Consider the following combinations of value and confidence and whether you've come across the kinds of folks described.

Table 3.1	Value and Confidence Examples	
VALUE	**CONFIDENCE**	**YOU'LL KNOW THESE PEOPLE BECAUSE . . .**
High	Low	These people are your fearful program participants. They're driven by their alignment with your program's purpose, but they're scared to death they will never be successful.
		When I picture these folks, I think about people entering public speaking programs. They choose to engage because speaking in front of a crowd matters to them. But their fear of failure and performing the very act they've come to learn is off the chart.[1]
Low	High	These people are often forced program participants. Whatever the program targets, they believe they're already capable—which may or may not be accurate. As a result, their value to engage is low.
		I first picture these people as the ones standing on the sidelines. They might be making critical comments under the general heading of "why bother." In some cases, they're even hostile program participants. Think about the people who are "forced" to go to professional development trainings for things they already know!
Low	Low	"I'm never going to be successful here, and I really don't care." That sums up these potential program participants.
		These people are experiencing the double motivation whammy. Picture someone being forced to take a class for which they have no interest and they know the subject matter is over their head.

[1]With good reason, since 75% of people rank *glossophobia* as their number one fear according to National Institutes of Mental Health.

VALUE	CONFIDENCE	YOU'LL KNOW THESE PEOPLE BECAUSE . . .
High	High	These people would seem to be the ideal. They care, and they're confident they will be successful. But remember that both value and confidence are intrinsic. These constructs stem from our own beliefs about ourselves. And it must be acknowledged that sometimes we're not objective judges of our own interests and abilities. The lesson here is to trust, but test for the true abilities. Are they right to be confident? Implementing a program that assumes confidence when it doesn't fully exist will quickly and negatively affect the motivation of your participants.

Another interesting thing about motivation and expectancy theory is this: Motivation is the *product* of value multiplied by confidence. Of course, this is a conceptual multiplication effort. But you'll undoubtedly note the application of a basic fact: Any number multiplied by zero is . . . zero. A-ha! It takes *both* value and confidence. For that very reason, our programs must carefully attend to both elements by nurturing them when already present or building them up when they're not.

DID YOU KNOW? THREE-BRAIN LEADERSHIP

The fact we humans each operate from three brains is one of the most fascinating findings the field of neuroscience has brought us in recent years. Sure, the mind–heart and mind–stomach connections have been theorized and even assumed to exist for ages. But recent insight about these connections has lead to some ground-breaking realizations about what compels our daily performance—including the countless decisions we make, many of which are made without conscious thought.

What are the **three brains?** The first is the one you expect. Termed the *cephalic* (or head) brain, it is responsible for cognition and thinking. It helpfully analyzes information, makes meaning, and leads us to decisions based on logic. The second is our *cardiac* or heart brain, and its contribution involves emotion. Here, think passion and compassion, core values, and more generally, our interpersonal relationships.

(Continued)

(Continued)

Finally, the *enteric* or gut brain, which takes the lead with intuition and regulating our sense of self.

It's pretty amazing when you think about it. When fears about being successful arise—say giving a speech in public for those with glossophobia—where is it felt? Naturally, in the gut! Your gut brain is ruling your sense of self and, in this case, confidence. When you feel compelled to do something—to learn a new skill, to volunteer for a worthy cause—where is it felt? That's your heart brain playing its part with emotions. In this case, feelings of value, which compel you to act.

Why is this all important to initiatives? First, I imagine you've already figured out that the three brains I've just described essentially map to the three barriers/strengths you've just learned. See what happened there? When we're working to figure out why something isn't happening as we'd like, we get to know the people involved—including understanding what they do/don't know (head brain), their current level of care related to the gap (heart brain), and their current level of confidence related to the gap (gut brain). Said another way, do they know it, do they care about it, and do they believe they can? All three brains must be not only engaged but on board and ready to go!

The Organization 4

The second two requisite elements that must be present for people to be successful are ones the organization controls. For educational leaders, these are things that may be within the control of you, at your school site, or others at the district level. Let's begin with incentives.

Incentives

This category is used to describe the things an organization offers in exchange for performance. Let's think broadly about the term **incentive** because it can take many forms: the grade a student gets for successfully performing in a class, the review an educator receives following a classroom observation, even the pay bump that comes with completing coursework or a degree. These are all examples of incentives. What do they share in common? Basically, someone external to the individual is offering a consequence in an overt way.

People often conclude that the word incentive is synonymous with money. While monetary compensation is always nice, there are many times when it isn't possible to provide. As school leaders, you're all too familiar with that challenge! So let's think broadly about incentives. Frankly, one of the best incentives available is one that is also arguably free: noticing and then saying something. The simple act of providing feedback can move mountains over time. To me, this is true largely because we rarely take the time to notice, let alone interact, about the simple things. Yet little gestures over time make for big differences—perhaps a brief conversation or an email saying I saw you doing this and I think it's great. They incentivize the "doing" and can really influence performance.

The final thing to remember about incentives is their relationship to motivation. Remember that motivation is intrinsic and the result of each person's own determination of their value and confidence. Incentives are extrinsic, which is why I picture them surrounding the people involved (as seen previously in Figure 2.1). When an incentive offered by the external source reaches the individual, the incentives may—or may not—impact their motivation. When they do, it's typically seen in the value component. When we're designing initiatives, we must be especially careful with the interplay between incentives and motivation. Misplaced incentives might quickly raise value, but in the wrong ways, as The Summer Institute vividly describes.

TALES FROM THE FIELD: THE SUMMER INSTITUTE

Some time ago, I evaluated a government-funded grant that was designed to increase classroom educator abilities to teach algebra. Through a multi-year, multi-component program design, teacher-participants would deepen their content knowledge while enhancing their pedagogical prowess to share that content with their students.

The program kicked off with a two week long Summer Institute. Interaction with pedagogy experts in algebra were combined with rich and contemporary teaching and learning strategies all in support of the program's ultimate goals: increasing teacher content knowledge and enhancing pedagogical practices, with the ultimate goal of students both learning more algebra and raising their value for its use, based on relevant, familiar examples.

All went well during summer, July to be exact. Teachers were paid, and rightly so—like any other professional—to attend the two-week program. They came, they engaged, and they talked about what they'd do in the coming school year.

Prior to winter break, we checked in with the participants as part of the program evaluation. While every last participant gave the program the highest marks and praise, less than 20% of them had applied their summer learnings in significant ways.

What I describe is common, in my experience, with professional learning efforts. I fully acknowledge that what happened here is the result of multiple factors, each of which could be nicely classified into one of our barrier/strength categories. But at a most basic level, it speaks to misplaced incentives. Think about it. What incentives did these teachers receive? If you're thinking pay for two weeks of their available, and valuable time—you're right. Pay for their time is right, no argument from me. But in providing that incentive and only that incentive, what outcome resulted? Was it the integration of deepened algebra content and enhanced pedagogy in their teaching? Unfortunately not. Rather, 10 days of summer institute attendance was incentivized.

What if, based on a plan of the teacher's own creation developed [at] the close of the summer institute, teachers were compensated for actually implementing their learnings in the classroom? Or lacking monetary options, what if program leaders connected with participants over time across the school year as an incentive for following through on their implementation commitments?

The moral of the story is rather simply this: Be very sure about how the incentive you offer influences the motivation of people involved in the initiative.

Environmental

Our final category of barriers/strengths attends to the **environment**. This is another "wrap around," pictured in Figure 2.1, that enables people to achieve the desired outcome. If we're going to be successful implementing technology-based instruction, we need the proper equipment and likely high-functioning Internet connections too.

But the environment category is a bit too broad; there are many barriers and strengths that fall into this area. Going back to Gilbert's model, it's helpful to break our considerations here into three areas: necessary tools and equipment, aligned policies and tactics expectations, and available time to perform. Table 4.1 provides examples from each of the three categories, which are likely recognizable to you.

Table 4.1 Environmental Barrier Examples		
TOOLS AND EQUIPMENT	**EXPECTATIONS**	**TIME**
Program requires high bandwidth Internet connection, while only limited speed is available

Teachers are trained on a new curriculum that isn't available until halfway through the school year | Outdated policy contradicts the very thing the program is expecting participants to do

Participants are expected to perform but lack control over the resources required to be successful | No time in the day to run program as expected

Competing priorities that lessen or eliminate application of the program content |

Summing Up Barriers and Strengths 5

You've just explored four categories which, together, underlie people's performance. Whether teaching decimal places, leading a LGBTIQA+ support group, or learning to apply a new acting technique, these elements serve to ensure your initiatives will have the results you seek.

Before we leave this topic, let's turn things 180 degrees. Take a moment and picture a program that *really* led to positive outcomes for you. It really could be anything. Maybe you were in 4-H, or Boy or Girl Scouts early in life. Perhaps you took an amazing photography course and now have framed masterpieces on the walls of your home. Or professionally, perhaps you took a career development course where your skills increased and you enjoyed the fruits of that growth applied on the job.

It doesn't matter which "program" you completed; walk yourself through the four categories that I have summarized in the table that follows by applying them to the program experience you're now picturing. Take an inventory of how each was present.

Successful initiatives attend to each of these things. I can pretty much guarantee that each was not only present but present in significant ways—assuming the experience you're contemplating was especially profound. This is why you'll be doing yourself a favor by considering these elements up front.

Consider . . .

- How can we make sure our participant not only has the necessary skill and knowledge but that they will be able to confidently apply it when the time comes?

- How will our participant come to find the program and its content relevant?

Table 5.1   Barrier and Strengths Definitions and Examples

CATEGORY	DEFINITION	EXAMPLES
Knowledge and skill	Possessing the necessary information and having sufficient opportunity to practice, to influence successful performance	Adequate training that also supports application of trained skills, over time, on-the-job Opportunity to practice and perfect involved performance Access to supports that target knowledge and skill, including coaching and reference guides
MOTIVATION	**VALUE** × **CONFIDENCE = MOTIVATION**	
Value	The import one ascribes to performing	Personal dedication to performing Held beliefs that performance will make a positive difference
Confidence	The beliefs one holds about whether they will or won't be successful	Measures of self-efficacy Held assumptions about whether they are capable of performing and the degree to which they will succeed if an attempt is made
Incentives	Things the organization offers that reward successful performance	Anything that the organization provides that signals a positive reinforcement for performance Often thought of as pay for performance, money Can be as simple as providing feedback This category also includes punitive measures as consequences for nonperformance
ENVIRONMENT	**COMPRISED OF TOOLS, EXPECTATIONS, AND TIME**	
Tools	Ready access to the tools and resources required for successful performance	Computers, programs, subscriptions Curriculum-required elements, like manipulatives References that can guide performance while it occurs
Expectations	Clear expectations, sometimes through policy, that align with successful performance	Directives that prioritize performance Policy that doesn't contradict performance
Time	Time required to perform is made available	The realistic and necessary time commitment is recognized and acknowledged Competing priorities are adjusted such that necessary time is available

- What will they need to take their learnings and successfully apply them?

- How will their success be recognized—by the individuals themselves and those around them?

I trust you'll begin to see that these elements are, at least slightly, magical. Sure, we can use them to assess the influences behind a gap. But we can also use them as a formula for what to bake into programs that bring about predictable success. That means these elements might be encountered as barriers to someone's performance, but they can also be used to drive performance toward success.

I'll leave you with the following visual that is designed to illustrate this two-pronged truth. You may encounter the four elements you've learned as barriers that are holding your participants back from reaching the optimal state. But as the initiative designer, you can also use these elements as drivers of performance. I've chosen to illustrate this as a tailwind at your future initiative participants' backs, pushing them toward the optimal state. If you've been on a plane, especially traveling a long distance, you know that having the tailwind gets you where you want to go . . . faster!

Figure 5.1   Barriers and Drivers Example

Barrier/Strength Categories as Barriers to Success: Incentives Example

Barrier/Strength Categories as Drivers to Success: Incentives Example

Let's Get Smart 6

You've taken time to consider the conceptual foundations of conducting a needs assessment as an initial step in the design of successful initiatives. We have explored definitions of gaps and influences (in the forms of barriers and strengths). I have shared examples to sharpen your ability to "know them when you see them." Now, let's take action in our initiative planning effort.

As I shared earlier, there are many reasons why people launch the planning process: achievement problems, mandated changes, exposure to great new ideas. Regardless of the impetus, your planning effort should begin by doing what I call *getting smart*. I use that term in pretty much the same way as *needs assessment*. But what I find is that getting smart is a bit more accurate in terms of what we're really doing at this stage. We're stepping back to consider what we've been asked to do (or have the opportunity to do) and consider it from *all sides* to understand the current situation, the opportunity, and what it will take to realize the vision.

How does all this relate to what you've learned about gaps and influencers? We've reached the point of taking action. Those concepts provide the template that your "getting smart" findings will populate. But more importantly, this stage of the work is essentially planning. You're building your understanding of the situation so that you can envision the initiative that will "fit" it—one that is responsive to the need and one that can move the needle in terms of benefits to the people and organization involved.

So let's turn our attention to seeking, finding, and organizing the information you need as you pursue, plan, and perfect this planning effort.

The 3Vs: Voice, Viewpoint, and Vision

As you begin your work documenting gaps and influences, I want to highlight a framework that can offer a set of lenses for your inquiry. I call them the **3Vs: voice, viewpoint, and vision**.

The 3Vs are a helpful set of lenses to "try on" as you plan and then work with your team and staff. Here are some key questions, aligned to each of the Vs, that can serve as iterative checks throughout your needs assessment data collection effort.

- Voice: Does your needs assessment fully represent the people involved in this situation or opportunity? If not, whose voice is missing to make this review equitable?

- Viewpoint: Are you gaining multiple perspectives? Have the data helped put you in a place where your own perspectives are set aside and you see things more like those involved?

- Vision: What data do you have that helps you understand anything about success through the eyes of the people involved or understand what programmatic solution might best serve and support your intended participants?

Monitor the incoming needs assessment data to identify where you've gained insight and what additional information and perspective you need for each of the 3Vs.

Finding and Minding the Gap

How do you uncover the gaps? Well, it requires getting into the shoes of the people involved.

So a primary gap has been defined—likely by you or another leader in your organization. Primary gaps can intimidate, frustrate, and sometimes obfuscate. Thus, it's best to begin with a careful investigation of the situation for purposes of detailing both the primary gap and the contributing gaps. You'll do this by adding detail to both the ideal and current components of the gap. And not to worry, there will be ample reminders to keep your appreciative lens on as well.

Beginning With What You Already (Can) Have

The good news with gap analysis is that you typically can find some existing information that helps us define and refine the gaps in play. Some examples are test scores, grades assigned, participation rates, number of people trained through professional development, teaching observations, and the list goes on depending on the situation you face. Starting with a **document review** (an analysis of existing materials of all kinds that help you understand the current or ideal states) makes sense for several reasons. First, it immediately makes you smarter about the situation. Second, as you build your understanding, you'll be able to ask better questions as you continue the investigation. Work with the easily accessible data and information to build your understanding of both the ideal and the current—which depends on the content of each piece of **extant data** (data you already have access to, usually gained during your document review).

Table 6.1 Examples of Existing Data	
EXISTING DATA TO . . . DESCRIBE THE CURRENT STATE	**EXISTING DATA TO . . . DESCRIBE THE IDEAL STATE**
• Test scores over time • Culture and climate surveys • Performance reviews • Usage data • Records of training received • Financial data • Parent feedback	• Documented performance goals • Stated compliance expectations • District- and school-level strategic plans • Education code

As you collect and review these data, make sure you're not setting anything aside simply because it is not adding to an understanding of a deficit. Yes—here is that appreciative lens. Is there an area where you're already exceeding the ideal state? Is there evidence of success or promise of success on any dimension of the situation you're investigating? Make sure to take careful note. In fact, you may want to note and circle it just to avoid becoming fully focused on solutions only focused on the deficits.

Taking the Search to the People

With the primary gap in mind and bolstered by your emerging understanding of the situation gained through your review of extant data, it's time to collect some data directly from the people involved. There are multiple ways to accomplish this that range from informal conversations to the more formal interviews and focus groups. Each of these approaches affords opportunities to ask questions, actively listen, and evolve the direction of your inquiry based on real-time responses. Surveys provide an alternate means for data collection with the potential to help you hear from a greater number of people in a relatively short amount of time.

Here is another interesting thing to try: Take a moment to picture the future. There is a successful initiative in place that you are now evaluating to fully describe its impact. What will that future program evaluation find and prove? Well, it is very likely to be evidence of the gaps you've closed through the design and implementation of your initiative! So as you go about this needs assessment and data collection—or consultation with your thought partners—remember that you're essentially defining the "needs" or requirements, which you'll then confirm having influenced when you reach the evaluation phase of the work. These needs assessment results will be useful for everything that lies ahead—from defining the program to establishing measurable outcomes and defining an evaluation plan that will demonstrate the program's value to your organization.

First Things First

Before engaging with the people involved, I suggest taking a deep dive to learn as much about the context as you can. Perhaps as the school or district leader you feel you know the context well. Yet, even in organizations you've served for years, there is often background material you've yet to review and process that can forward your efforts. Take a moment to consider whether this situation is true for you and whether there are new ways in which you could understand your organization and its inevitable layers before you start collecting data. Your goal is to develop fresh eyes with which to see and understand the situation.

Framing Good Needs Assessment Questions

Having developed or bolstered your knowledge about the situation through existing sources, it is likely time to speak with the folks who are involved. You will want to speak with a variety of people that includes those who oversee and influence the situation, as well as a representative sample of those who will be active participants in the initiative you design.

Reviewing the Players

In all cases, you will want to consult with the person I call the *leader or key leader*. This is the person who has challenged you to address the identified gap. Questions here should revolve around how the need for this initiative came about and how, in the broadest sense, it should benefit the organization. Work to fully understand the initial driver that gave rise to this new-found need for action, and keep it in mind as you continue your needs assessment data collection. Site leaders typically collaborate with those at the district level, so your "key leader" may reside there. If you're a site leader and fully fueling the initiative, I encourage you to reflect on these same questions. When you're close to the situation, it is important to regularly check your objectivity by comparing your growing understanding with the original need that launched your efforts.

Touching base with folks I will term **thought partners** at this stage is also helpful. These are folks whose support you're going to need to implement the program. A diverse group of thought partners may share equally diverse perspectives on situation, needs, and possible solutions. Documenting the range of needs upfront ensures that your eventual initiative plan will accommodate the involvement of and support from the full range of necessary supporters.

Finally, you must benefit from speaking with members of your intended participant group or groups. These are the folks who will become active participants in your initiative. Certainly, they can provide you with helpful context about the primary gap and what it is like to stand in their shoes, here in the current state. Becoming acquainted at this stage will help you begin to determine the types of strategies your initiative might involve. For example, now is a good time to note literacy and language abilities, access to and ability with technology, and any other limitations and accelerators that stand to impact program design.

Asking the Right Questions

You are beginning to see the benefits of accomplishing this up-front planning effort. We have discussed an initial "getting smart" phase of your work. That phase is typically accomplished prior to detailed meetings with any of the folks involved because it readies you to ask the right questions.

It also allows you to walk into those conversations and demonstrate your commitment to and care for the situation. You're taking a keen interest in this challenge, and your established knowledge about it will demonstrate that to each person whose input you invite.

Next, it's time to take the initial understanding you've gained by "getting smart" and engage more deeply with the people involved. This effort will help you "fill in the blanks" for missing information you likely identified in your "getting smart" review. It will also allow you to ask good questions about needs and opportunities. Finally, this phase provides an unprecedented opportunity for you to begin building trust with the people your initiative will involve—both supporters and intended participants. Demonstrating your interest and care helps you gain the trust you need for people to open up and "tell it like it is." Ultimately, even the most expertly planned initiative will be compromised if you fail to achieve the necessary support for your work from the people who surround the proposed program.

The 3Vs Up Close

We've introduced the 3Vs, so let's take a moment to further define what we mean by each.

Voice involves giving voice to or amplifying the voice of *all* people involved in whatever situation or opportunity your efforts are driving. It means intentionally inviting the sharing of voices and then listening attentively. It also means ensuring representation of all voices with attention to balancing their volume.

Viewpoints means working to understand where the involved people stand and how the situation looks and feels from their unique perspectives or viewpoints. Certainly, it is impossible to fully understand, appreciate, and share the lived experience of each person involved. But we must set an intention to develop such understandings, within the limitations of time and other resources available, because they directly influence everything from elements of motivation to skills- and knowledge-related solutions and beyond.

Vision includes what success would look like and what it would take to achieve as envisioned by the very people your initiative will involve. While a leader or some other external force may have coined the gap, it is the people involved who will ultimately determine whether the designed or selected program achieves full implementation and has lasting results. Therefore, it only makes sense to document the vision of those involved.

As you investigate needs during the program planning effort, use the 3Vs as a north star. The more you understand the people involved, the better your initiative can reflect their needs and aspirations.

	TOOL 1: REALIZING THE 3V'S—VOICE, VIEWPOINTS, AND VISION
Purpose	Develop effective questions to use for planning the evaluation effort with key leaders, thought partners, and potential participants.
Task	Use this tool to brainstorm relevant questions to use when initially working with key leaders and thought partners.

	CONSIDERATIONS AND STRATEGIES FOR . . .
Voice	• Think broadly about *all* of the people who could benefit from your program and make a list.
	• Reviewing your list, brainstorm ways you can make sure you hear from every type of person and group on the list.
	• Recognize that people differ in the ways they're willing and able to share their voices.
	• Consider what would be the ideal means for gaining and amplifying voices of each potential participant profile demographic.
	• Provide an array of opportunities for intended initiative participants to contribute—from listening sessions to surveys and interviews to the means for anonymous input.
	• Recognize that you, yourself, might not be the ideal person to seek voice from people in each of your potential participant groups—consider whether folks will be open and candid with you or whether you should enlist the support of someone with whom they may be more open.
Viewpoint	• Acknowledge that you own lived experience will differ, perhaps greatly, from that of your future participants.
	• Check your positionality and adopt strategies to keep it in check as you invite input.
	• Dedicate yourself to understanding lived experiences, specific to needs and the challenge at hand.
	• Ask clarifying questions and pose scenarios and examples to hone your emerging understanding of their viewpoint.
	• Guard against and reject impulses to interpret the viewpoints of others—especially those who differ greatly from yourself—based on your own reality.
	• Assume what you're hearing from an intended participant is fact—because, from their reality, it is exactly that, regardless of contradictory information you may hold.
	• Ask questions and encourage continued sharing to understand the knowledge and beliefs that underlie stated viewpoints.
Vision	• Invite intended participants to create the program by asking what they would do to share their ideals, their dreams.
	• Use these shared visions to further understand viewpoints by working to understand the interplay between shared viewpoints and visions.
	• Respect any and all visions and ideas shared with you.

(Continued)

(Continued)

	CONSIDERATIONS AND STRATEGIES FOR . . .
	• Resist any statement, action, or body language that could be interpreted as dismissing a shared vision or idea.
	• Assume all shared ideas, including solutions, hold merit.
	• Ask clarifying questions to deepen understanding of both the shared vision and the beliefs that underlie that vision—the what and the why.

Next, let's look at some questions that can help you investigate the opportunity before you. Having benefited from the earliest review of extant data that helped you understand context, you likely will already possess answers to some of the questions that follow. If you do, great! The emerging understanding will help guide your further investigation, as you pose questions to everyone involved.

Tool 2 offers a range of questions for the typical folks you would consult, to help you frame this important stage of need assessment inquiry.

TOOL 2: ASKING GOOD QUESTIONS

Purpose	Develop effective questions to use for needs assessment queries with thought partners, supporters, and potential participants.
Task	Use this tool to brainstorm relevant questions for use when initially exploring gaps with thought partners, supporters, and potential participants.

NEEDS

- What led you to select or seek to develop this initiative?
- What do you hope to accomplish through this initiative? In the short-term? Ultimately, over time?
- Are there already defined outcomes for this effort? If not, can you describe the outcomes you hope it will achieve?
- What are some of the reasons these types of outcomes aren't already occurring?

PROGRAM OPERATION

- How do you see the initiative being implemented?
- On what timeline should the initiative occur?
- What challenges do you anticipate we might encounter implementing the initiative/using the initiative?
- What are some indicators you use to determine if the initiative is "on track"?

IDEAL RESULTS

- If we could fast forward to a point where the initiative's success was evident, what would we see? How would we know the initiative "worked?"

- What kinds of things would you find helpful to know about the initiative and its impact?

- What types of evidence would you consider persuasive?

- What benefits should participants be able to describe after participating in/using the initiative?

- In what ways would our organization and future efforts look different if this initiative is successful?

TALES FROM THE FIELD: WHY NOW?

I'll admit it. I absolutely love doing needs assessments. Sometimes, it makes me feel like a detective as I pursue clues, weigh evidence, and work to make perfect sense out of a challenging situation. Other times, it makes me feel like the kind of doctor (medial) my parents likely wish I'd become. I assess symptoms, ponder diagnoses and differential diagnoses, all the while positing what will truly "cure" the challenge we face—rather than simply treating the symptoms. Finally, needs assessments give me the chance to apply my best learned skills as one-part organizational therapist and another part organizational intuitive, to look at a situation with fresh eyes and help everyone involved make meaning. I see every one of these skills as contributing to my success, regardless of whose career choice I'm choosing to imagine on any given day.

But do you want to know a really big secret? Alright—here it is: Almost always, the most telling questions you can ask are the following:

- How did this situation come about?

- Why now?

Seems simple. But if you're posing those questions to the right people, you may be surprised how much you learn.

First, let's cover finding the right person. Perhaps, needless to say, if the answer is something like "Because my boss said we gotta do it," then you've not yet found the right person. I had a colleague who referred to

(Continued)

(Continued)

those folks as "order takers," seemingly comparing them to the helpful people you might find in your favorite restaurant. They're basically bringing about what was ordered. So if your question is answered by an order taker, time to move a step higher in your school or district.

There are two specific things you're looking for at this high-level stage of questioning. First, you're trying to tease out how this need and press for a solution has come about at this point in time. Second, take note of consensus . . . or lack thereof. If everyone tells you something different, that may signal an additional need to bring people together.

When I've asked this question, I've heard some amazing things. Of course, my favorite is that "The superintendent saw the program at a conference and really liked it. They bought it on the spot. Now, we've got to figure out what to do with it." Note how that, at face value, is a program looking for a need!

Another common response from leaders at the site level goes something like this: "Well, the central office said every school needs to be part of the STEM initiative, but we can all figure out what that means for us." This one is a bit concerning because I'm pretty sure there isn't as much latitude in that freedom when push comes to shove, and results aren't forthcoming.

Helpful responses include those that smack of strategy. For example, I've heard "Two years ago, we adopted our zero-tolerance bullying policy. Yet the number of incidents hasn't declined as much as we'd like. We need to figure out whether to evolve that policy or how to better support it with programs in order to see the reduction we want." Now that, you can work with.

Answers to these early questions, including perspectives from high-level leaders, can provide keen insight into challenges you're about to pursue through an initiative. Take the time to ask these important questions and allow the responses to guide your thinking and further quest for data.

Collecting Needs Assessment Data 7

Information is all around us. The availability of data only continues to grow. It is fueled by technology innovation and what seems like an endless range of opportunities to "track" things. From the more traditional data sources—like test scores and regularly collected survey data—to more unique data streams—like usage figures, web traffic, even social media and sentiment analysis—we face more sources than any one initiative can use.

I've suggested you begin your quest for data with what already "is." That means leveraging the existing data that surrounds you—or can surround you—in support of developing your initial understanding of the people, the gaps, and the influences. Start by taking an inventory of what's already known about the challenge or opportunity. You might also tap your own close network of colleagues and query them about where they'd look to get smarter. With some creative thinking, you might be surprised what comes up.

Prioritizing Perspectives You Don't Already Have

Once you have reviewed the range of existing data, it's time to take stock of what you still need to hear and know. Remember the 3Vs here. Our goal is to fully understand the situation and ultimately build a program that reflects our staff and community. Where possible and practical, it should be a participatory process. The program you develop shouldn't be a surprise to anyone involved. Instead, the goal is for those you lead to say things like "Oh, this is that program we gave input about" or "Wow, they took our ideas seriously."

But imagine being asked for your opinion and ideas only to have them promptly ignored or discounted. Certainly the person who said, "There are no bad ideas," realized that idea was undoubtedly bad. But the inverse line of thinking, essentially, "All ideas are good," is equally true—and perhaps to a greater degree. By intently listening to those involved, we can begin to understand things through their voices, views, and visions. If some data point or perspective arises that immediately seems off base, delay your judgment. Assume all perspectives hold value and find some within what is shared, even if at first it seems difficult. If nothing else, suspend your disbelief for a time and allow it to share mind space with the other data you collect. You may be surprised how that contrarian idea comes to shape your understanding.

You have now well-positioned yourself to receive these perspectives. Next, you must go out and get them.

Data Questing

There are a finite number of formalized ways by which we can invite people to share ideas and perspectives. Each has benefits and each has limitations. Let's consider the use of surveys, interviews, and focus groups as strategies for understanding gaps, causes, and capabilities from our participant's perspective. We'll also add observations and extant data as potential sources, simply to offer an at-a-glance listing of data collection methods that can guide your planning.

TOOL 3: COLLECTION METHODS TO CONSIDER	
Purpose	Define a range of data collection methods that can be used in both needs assessment and program evaluation.
Task	Use this tool to brainstorm, and then weigh the benefits and limitations of a range of data collection methods.
METHOD	**DESCRIPTION AND GUIDANCE**
Questionnaires and Surveys	Used to record participant attributes (i.e., demographics), perspectives, experiences, intentions, beliefs, and more. Surveys can be tricky to design such that they receive valid and reliable data that can successfully inform your planning. I share a note about "leading with surveys" following.

METHOD	DESCRIPTION AND GUIDANCE
Interview	A flexible tool that provides for adjustment of questions by the interviewer "on the fly." Helpful for in-depth exploring of situations, experiences, and opinions. Provides opportunities for the interviewer to press deeper as necessary.
Focus Group	People sometimes consider a focus group to be the equivalent of a group interview. But the goal of a focus group is conversation among the participants. A focus group is helpful for exploring an idea or experience, as well as pressing to see whether consensus can be achieved by the group around a given topic.
Observation	Observation can be informal or driven by a pre-established protocol. A formalized observation can be useful for determining the frequency of behaviors, confirming levels of participation, and so forth. Often, multiple observations are necessary to develop an accurate picture of a given phenomenon.
Assessment	Typically used to test the skills or knowledge of participants, confirming current levels of skill or ability. Can take the form of a constructed response instrument (i.e., multiple choice test) or an authentic demonstration of applied knowledge or skills (on-the-job performance assessment).

Knowing When to Survey

A reminder about the oft-used survey is warranted. Remember to assess whether you know enough about the situation to construct a valid survey. Surveys are helpful tools when you know enough to anticipate a range of responses and accommodate those responses on the survey page. Remember that if your survey ends up being largely open-ended questions, it's likely you should be doing interviews or even focus groups rather than surveys. Surveys are an especially good way to hear from many people. Analysis can often be done more rapidly, relative to qualitative interview data. Yet that doesn't necessarily make the survey the ideal data collection tool in every situation.

That said, conducting interviews with some of your staff followed by a survey of the larger group of involved people, for example, can be a powerful approach, especially when the interviews deepen your early understanding such that you can construct an effective survey.

TALES FROM THE FIELD: TAKING STOCK OF WHAT YOU ALREADY (CAN) KNOW

Sometimes the data we already have can push our need assessment inquiry dramatically forward. Taking stock of what you already know or can know is well worth the time it requires, given the things you stand to learn.

Here's a great example. I was recently working with some district leaders on a social-emotional learning opportunity. With the early recognition that *all* learning is social-emotional, they had noticed their established program had faltered during the pandemic. I asked them to share with me how they had concluded that the program had indeed faltered. Believe it or not, they told me their analytics showed it.

Analytics? At first blush, that sounded far away from anything related to social-emotional learning. Yet some quick and basic analysis of online interaction allowed them to pinpoint a gap around digital citizenship that was largely about asynchronous communication. They pulled rich examples to instantiate the challenge. They also took the time to look for digital citizenship-related outcomes as well as larger social emotional outcomes that were being demonstrated with success through the same digital records. By dedicating the time to document the capabilities, they surfaced the existing, successful foundation on which their program solution might naturally build and reach the point of positive impact more quickly. The lesson is simply this: By asking around and getting creative with their analysis of existing data, their understanding of the current challenge swiftly grew. Were there limitations to this approach? Absolutely. But the limited time investment was well worth the new insights realized through this extent data analysis.

Coming Closer to Clarity 8

Summarizing Needs

Successful needs assessment efforts yield plenty of data. Sometimes we're faced with more data than we can possibly use. When such conditions arise, I challenge myself to prioritize the available data. I will admit, I'm prejudiced here when it comes to giving more weight to all information that comes directly from the participants involved. This is probably, in part, due to the fact I've encountered (and experienced) many programs that were "done to me" rather than "done with me." The risks here are many, but chief among them is developing something based on your assumptions that fully miss the mark. When we privilege information from the very people involved, we serve to mitigate that "done to me" risk.

Reaching Clarity

At this stage, you'll consider the conversations you've had, the documents you've reviewed, and the unique setting every organization provides in which leaders must operate. It is here that I'm reminded of one of my favorite quotes that, when I first heard it, was ascribed to an ancient philosopher from some unknown region of Asia:

> *Your mind is like water, my friend. When it is agitated, it becomes difficult to see. But if you allow it to settle, the answer becomes clear.*

I trust you, like me, will find truth in this analogy. It's only when all the "inputs" are given time to settle that you can make meaning and see a path forward. First, give yourself time to reflect—and *reflect* before you *react*. Time is a critical ingredient to reaching clarity. Oh, one other thing about this helpful analogy: After professing both quote and origin, as I earlier described, to my doctoral students for any number of years, one day I decided to try to cite the definitive source. It was then I learned that the "ancient philosopher" isn't so ancient: The quote is attributed to Po, who you might better know as . . . Kung Fu Panda. Regardless, the analogy sticks!

Organizing Your Data

In the next section of this book, you will formally begin processing data and connecting needs, barriers, and strengths to elements of the initiatives you're beginning to shape. Before you do that and in this moment of coming to clarity about what you've learned, I'd encourage you to write the headlines. Sure, you likely have rich data that quickly deepens any needs assessment headline. Having that data is undoubtedly a plus and something you will reference in both the design and evaluation stages of your effort. But boiling things down to a set of **needs assessment headlines** helps summarize your findings and offers an initial step in making them actionable and disseminating them to everyone involved.

Use Tool 4 to guide your summarizing effort.

TOOL 4: NEEDS ASSESSMENT HEADLINE AUTHORING TOOL	
Purpose	Summarize findings into a finite set of headlines that describe the need in tangible terms.
Task	Use this tool to summarize the key findings of your needs assessment. Think about your team and others interested in your initiative planning effort and use language that will be familiar and persuasive to them.
THE GAP	
Primary Gap	Describe the top-level gap—using needs assessment evidence.
	Example headline: While all third-grade students should perform at the "proficient" level or above, 80% of English learners across our district are scoring "below proficient" on the annual state test.
	Your headline:

THE GAP

Contributing Gaps	Describe other identified gaps that you believe are influencing the primary gap.
	Example headlines:
	Our school values parent involvement: Overall, approximately 80% of parents engage with their child's teacher at least four times a year; the rate for parents of English learners is less than 16%.
	Twenty-seven percent of parents of English learners (EL) indicate they read with their children at least once a week, whereas all parents should be engaging in at-home reading.
	Use of the district's online language arts curriculum has been declining over the past three years, to the point where fewer than one third of EL students are logging in weekly.
	Your headlines:

BARRIERS AND STRENGTHS

List each headline that follows and then describe the barriers and/or strengths that are influencing (causing) the situation.

EXAMPLE GAP	CATEGORY	EXAMPLE BARRIER/STRENGTH DESCRIPTION
Headline 1 Example headline: *While all third-grade students should perform at the "proficient" level or above, 80% of English learners across our district are scoring "below proficient" on the annual state test.*	Skills and Knowledge	Example barrier: *Students lack the necessary skills/abilities to read at proficient level.*
	Value and Confidence	Example barrier: *Interviews with students indicate low levels of confidence: "Every time I think I'm doing better, I get a lower score, I'm never going to learn this."*
	Incentives	Example: *No barriers/strengths*
	Expectations, Tools, and Time	Example strength: *Students know the expectation is grade-level reading proficiency.* Example strength: *The district has invested in an online reading program that targets ELs in particular.*

(Continued)

(Continued)

HEADLINE	CATEGORY	BARRIER/STRENGTH DESCRIPTION
	Skills and Knowledge	
	Value and Confidence	
	Incentives	
	Expectations, Tools, and Time	
HEADLINE	**CATEGORY**	**BARRIER/STRENGTH DESCRIPTION**
	Skills and Knowledge	
	Value and Confidence	
	Incentives	
	Expectations, Tools, and Time	
HEADLINE	**CATEGORY**	**BARRIER/STRENGTH DESCRIPTION**
	Skills and Knowledge	
	Value and Confidence	
	Incentives	
	Expectations, Tools, and Time	
HEADLINE	**CATEGORY**	**BARRIER/STRENGTH DESCRIPTION**
	Skills and Knowledge	
	Value and Confidence	
	Incentives	
	Expectations, Tools, and Time	
HEADLINE	**CATEGORY**	**BARRIER/STRENGTH DESCRIPTION**
	Skills and Knowledge	
	Value and Confidence	
	Incentives	
	Expectations, Tools, and Time	

Wrap-Up for Part I
Linda's Needs in Focus

Seems like just the other day, Linda—the elementary district's lead professional learning coordinator you met a while back—was telling me how they had just completed this process. She was addressing a request from her superintendent to put a formal family engagement program in place. I noted how she didn't use the pronoun "I," which immediately made me happy. Linda made space at the table for people to share, provide input, and contribute to shared understanding.

Needs Assessment Steps

Here are some of the highlights that describe what Linda's team did.

1. **First, Linda formed a 15-member needs assessment team.** Site leaders, teachers, members of her professional learning group, parents, and community partners joined the team. Linda made them feel involved, helped them connect to the effort, and gave them responsibilities to ignite their investment and participation.

2. **The team began by meeting with the superintendent, asking questions, and doing a lot of listening.** When asked, "Why now?" the superintendent explained that increasing family engagement was a long-term, unaddressed goal for the district. They'd worked on developing leaders, optimizing curriculum, and enhancing technology-based learning. It was high time the district reached out to families.

3. **The team developed a rapid feedback tool to quantify the number of family focused events and typical attendance percentages for each.** Each site leader responded with those metrics that gave the team a very good understanding of the two actuals.

4. **Then, they added the parent voice.** It would have been nice to just write a survey and send it to every parent, but they didn't know the right questions to ask. So they interviewed 60 parents (four parents per team member) using open-ended questions that were guided by the 3Vs (voice, viewpoint, vision). Then, they took what they learned and successfully produced a survey to expand the interview findings with a larger sample of parent voices.

5. **As the team reached out to the community to drum up survey responses, they also took the opportunity to informally gather information from community partners.** Conversational questions explored current school connections, unmet opportunities for engagement, and avenues through which the district could work with community partners to engage parents and realize the multiplicative benefits that could result.

6. **After reflecting on learnings from parents and community members, the team reached out to teachers.** Here, using a well-crafted survey, they queried teachers about their efforts to engage families—including their strategies and frequency of engagement. Teachers shared what was working and what gets in the way.

7. **And finally, using the survey results, they identified teachers across the district who appeared to be doing amazing things in the area of family engagement.** After all, if great things were happening in areas of the district, they should be understood and considered for expansion across the district—as potential best practices.

Linda was very deliberate in interpreting and understanding the finding about actuals. "Of course, you realize that data right there mostly tells us how many ways we're trying to invite families, how consistent those ways are across the district, and a reasonable guess at how many families are responding. So many would stop here—and that would be exactly the *wrong* thing to do. At that point, we hadn't even talked to one family! I did have people on my team who are parents in the district, and it would have been easy to rely on their perspectives for the voice of the family, almost like 'double agents!' But, of course, that isn't the typical parent—if there is such a thing. So, our needs assessment pressed forward."

What the Team Gained

One of the things I was curious about was how the team saw the return on investment (ROI) in this needs assessment effort. Linda purposefully involved 15 people in this early phase so that they could distribute the time-intensive work. But beyond that, two other key things happened:

- **First, the team developed direct lines of communication—with schools, parents, and community partners.** She called these people "thought partners" and suggested that their input was not only valuable up-front but would be invited as the initiative took shape. By engaging this group early on, they would become champions for the initiative when the time came to roll it out across the district.

- **Second, Linda put her team of 15 on the front lines.** Each of them went out, collected data, put feet to pavement, and interacted with parents and community partners. The team's lived experience was critical to interpreting the needs assessment data, helping team members see the value of their contributions in exchange for their investments of time, and sustaining their participation in this work as things moved to initiative design. And they all stuck around as a result.

Needs Assessment Findings

As Linda and her team finished up, here is a look at their findings summarized in the needs assessment headline authoring tool.

FINDINGS FROM LINDA'S EFFORT: NEEDS ASSESSMENT HEADLINE AUTHORING TOOL	
THE GAP	
Primary Gap	Across the district, site leaders estimate that, on average, less than 47% of parents having meaningful interactions with their child's school—beyond pick-up/drop-off or handling attendance matters—each year. The average participation number varies widely by school; schools with high English learner populations have the lowest interaction rates (~ < 23%), followed by schools with high BIPOC enrollments (~ < 36%).

(Continued)

(Continued)

FINDINGS FROM LINDA'S EFFORT: NEEDS ASSESSMENT HEADLINE AUTHORING TOOL		
THE GAP		
Contributing Gap(s)	• When asked about family engagement, many (72%) teachers point to a variety of events that are held throughout the year—most often open houses and parent-teacher conferences—as their primary opportunities for engaging parents. There is no planned, coordinated, and consistent effort, with expectations, across the district. • Parent surveys confirm the teacher perspective, where open houses (88%) and conferences (65%) are most often viewed as the sole opportunities for engagement. • There are significant differences in how comfortable parents feel interacting with staff in their child's school. Here, parents of BIPOC students are two times less likely to indicate being comfortable, and parents of English learners are five times less likely to indicate being comfortable.	
BARRIERS AND STRENGTHS		
HEADLINE	**CATEGORY**	**BARRIER/STRENGTH DESCRIPTION**
Across the district, site leaders estimate that, on average, less than 47% of parents having meaningful interactions with their child's school—beyond pick-up/drop-off or handling attendance matters—each year. The average participation number varies widely by school; schools with high English learner populations have the lowest interaction rates (~ < 23%), followed by schools with high BIPOC enrollments (~ < 36%).	Skills and Knowledge	Many parents describe not knowing how to engage with the school or their child's teacher. They say they know nothing about education and don't know how to begin the conversations.
	Value and Confidence	Parents indicate a lack of confidence in being successful engaging with educators and leaders at their child's school. They fear they will "look stupid," "say something wrong," or "not be able to share their concerns so that they are understood." Teachers share that reaching out to parents often brings in more of the same parents they're already hearing from . . . "So, why even try?"
	Incentives	Some parents suggest that they have tried to become more involved in their child's education, but they've been turned away or turned off by the reaction of their child's teacher and left feeling like they don't belong.

BARRIERS AND STRENGTHS		
HEADLINE	**CATEGORY**	**BARRIER/STRENGTH DESCRIPTION**
	Expectations, Tools, and Time	Teachers say there is no time in the day to reach out to parents beyond what they're already doing—which many feel is sufficient. There is currently no expectation to run a specific family engagement effort. That said, the district has made great progress in building the capacity of leaders and selecting new curriculum—including curriculum with family connections. These developments can directly support the future family engagement initiative.
HEADLINE	**CATEGORY**	**BARRIER/STRENGTH DESCRIPTION**
When asked about family engagement, many (72%) teachers point to a variety of events that are held throughout the year—most often open houses and parent-teacher conferences—as their primary opportunities for engaging parents. There is no planned, coordinated, and consistent effort, with expectations, across the district.	Skills and Knowledge	While teachers appear to be well-versed in parent *events*—open houses and conferences—many lack an understanding of a more comprehensive and intentional approach to engage parents and sustain their engagement across a full school year.
	Value and Confidence	Roughly half of the teachers surveyed were aware of the connection between academic achievement and family engagement. This is likely a stronghold that could be leveraged for the initiative. In the absence of a formalized program, teachers are left to do whatever they wish, and many either feel they're doing enough or lack the confidence to try something new, where they might fail.

(Continued)

(Continued)

BARRIERS AND STRENGTHS		
HEADLINE	**CATEGORY**	**BARRIER/STRENGTH DESCRIPTION**
	Incentives	Teacher evaluations do not currently include expectations nor performance measures that address family engagement.
	Expectations, Tools, and Time	Again, time is seen as a barrier with teachers challenging the addition of one more thing to their fully allocated day.
HEADLINE	**CATEGORY**	**BARRIER/STRENGTH DESCRIPTION**
Parent surveys confirm the teacher perspective, where open houses (88%) and conferences (65%) are most often viewed as the sole opportunities for engagement.	Skills and Knowledge	Teachers believe they are engaging parents, but "all I can do is ask them to come . . . the choice is theirs." When pressed for strategies they might use to increase participation, teachers most often suggested that communicating the opportunity was the extent of their efforts: "They should want to come."
	Value and Confidence	—
	Incentives	Teachers have no formal expectation for engaging parents. Therefore, what is done under the general category of "family engagement" varies greatly from one teacher to the next. The lack of expectation results in many teachers choosing not to pursue opportunities other than the two required events.
	Expectations, Tools, and Time	When asked what keeps them from engaging in these existing opportunities, parents reported conflicts with their work hours, lack of transportation, and the need for childcare.

BARRIERS AND STRENGTHS		
HEADLINE	CATEGORY	BARRIER/STRENGTH DESCRIPTION
There are significant differences in how comfortable parents feel interacting with staff in their child's school. Here, parents of BIPOC students are two times less likely to indicate being comfortable, and parents of English learners are five times less likely to indicate being comfortable.	Skills and Knowledge	Many parents lack the knowledge of how to engage with staff in their child's school. In some cases, they didn't finish K–12 themselves and therefore don't have the understanding that comes from the schooling experience.
	Value and Confidence	While parents overall have a desire to support their children and make them successful in school, their lack of comfort engaging with school staff regularly overrides acting upon their desire. Interestingly, when the source of the parent survey invitation was tracked, we found that more than 33% of responding parents heard about the survey through the community and less than 66% of parents responded via the school request. This may be influenced by their lack of comfort and confidence engaging with the school.
	Incentives	Some parents see open houses and parent-teacher conferences as confrontative, having had bad experiences in the past. For example, "It's always bad news, never good, when I walk into that school."
	Expectations, Tools, and Time	—

What of a World Where None of This Happened?

What if the team had just made some assumptions based on their own understanding? Usually that approach yields loosely defined programs that have no true "root" in the school or district.

- The team would have missed the fact that teachers see open houses and conferences as parent engagement—a viewpoint that needs shifting.

- They wouldn't have known about the connection between the superintendent's efforts to date, building leaders and reforming curricula, and how that could directly connect to this initiative.

- And the parents—the very people this initiative is designed to engage—would have had absolutely no voice. They'd end up with a parent engagement program done *to* them rather than *with* them. Wouldn't that be ironic?

The last thing I'll share with you now, about this example, is this: When you see a deck of PowerPoint slides quickly fashioned and a district-wide in-service scheduled to "train people up" on family engagement, recognize that such an effort is the exact opposite of the initiative focus I want to see you adopt. And how many in-services have we been to where absolutely nothing changed? Initiatives, grounded in fully understood needs, lead to predictable change and results. Count on it.

PART I: DISCUSSION QUESTIONS

Use these questions to check your understanding or share your learnings with your initiative team.

1. Why is a needs assessment an important first step in the design of any initiative?

2. How would you define the term *opportunity gap?*

3. What does appreciative inquiry contribute to the needs assessment process—and, potentially, to the initiative design overall?

4. What are the four performance drivers that underlie any initiative participant's potential to successfully reach an initiative's outcomes?

5. What considerations should be made when deciding whether to use interviews or surveys as a data collection method?

6. What are the potential consequences of proceeding to initiative design without first dedicating time to a needs assessment?

PACING YOUR NEEDS ASSESSMENT EFFORT

I'm well-aware that the life of a leader is one of many responsibilities and priorities and limited time to fulfill the many expectations you face. Adding a comprehensive, multistep needs assessment effort—similar to the one I've described that Linda and her team pursued—may not be a reality you're able to fully stomach. Of course, you'll also likely run up against the natural urge and possible peer pressure to spend your available time "doing, not studying."

How should you proceed when you know a careful needs assessment is the "right" thing to do but the realities of time and available resources simply won't allow it?

Short answer: Some needs assessment is better than none, and a needs assessment need not always be comprehensive and deep to hold value.

Long answer: While my experience has proven that a careful and complete needs assessment is the ideal, almost any amount of a needs assessment will put you on better ground compared to doing none at all. The one caveat is this: No matter the size of the effort, you must make certain the data you collect accurately depicts the situation.

Table 8.1 provides some advice about needs assessments that should help you plot the "right" course for your initiative.

(Continued)

(Continued)

Table 8.1 Planning Your Needs Assessment Investment	
IF YOU'RE ABLE TO INVEST	**HERE'S WHAT I RECOMMEND YOU DO FOR A NEEDS ASSESSMENT**

One Day	1. Begin by defining the optimal state—in other words, first get clear on where you're heading.
	
	2. Spend a half-day going over every piece of extant data you can find that makes you smarter about the current challenge.
	
	3. Then, get out and simply talk to people who are involved in the challenge:
	
	  a. With limited time, focus mostly on hearing from the primary people who are involved instead of casting a wider net to include those who are on the periphery.
	
	  b. Use the 3Vs and Asking Good Questions tools to frame some questions, and ask them to as many people as you can find.
	
	  c. Listen for (a) evidence that helps define the current state and (b) reasons why the optimal state hasn't been reached.
	
	4. Take a final hour to summarize what you've learned using the Headline Authoring Tool, which will help you prepare for initiative design.

One Week	Use the one-day ideas, but also consider these additional ideas.
	
	1. Bring together a team to surface ideas you'll want to explore in your needs assessment.
	
	2. Expand the amount and types of inquiry:
	
	  a. Reach further for extant data of all kinds—including requesting data or reports that aren't immediately at-hand.
	
	  b. In addition to those who are the target of your initiative, work to understand the situation from the perspectives of others that will be involved in the implementation.

IF YOU'RE ABLE TO INVEST	HERE'S WHAT I RECOMMEND YOU DO FOR A NEEDS ASSESSMENT
	c. Consider surveys use so that you can hear from more people while also benefitting from interviews or a focus group for deeper dives. 3. Dedicate one day to review, interpret, reflect upon, and then summarize the data. 4. Dedicate a half-day to presenting results to a team of thought partners for additional perspectives, then use your thought partners to brainstorm possible solutions.
A Month+	Use the one-day and one-week ideas, but also consider these additional ideas: 1. Invest time in building a team of initiative thought partners and needs assessment data collectors, similar to what Linda did. 2. Catalog all extant data that stands to inform your work, request it, and then review it. 3. Plan and then conduct a robust data collection effort that gives voice to future participants, implementors, and leadership whose support the initiative must have: • Consider a sequential data collection approach that beings with the big picture, often through broad surveying, and then moves toward uncovering the more nuanced picture through interviews of focus groups. 4. Allocate at least a week to both analyze the data and give the team time to process and reflect on what it means. 5. Meet regularly with team to discuss progress, learnings to-date, and next steps. 6. Summarize findings and recommendations in an easy-to-read, data-based needs assessment report that will resonate with leaders whose support you must have.

PART II

Designing and Launching the Initiative

Through initiatives, education leaders orchestrate the necessary parts, people, processes—and then perform, much like the conductor of a symphony. Carefully planned initiatives put into action are like the beautiful music that results when players are on the same page, carefully executing their part but all the while collaborating under the leadership the conductor provides.

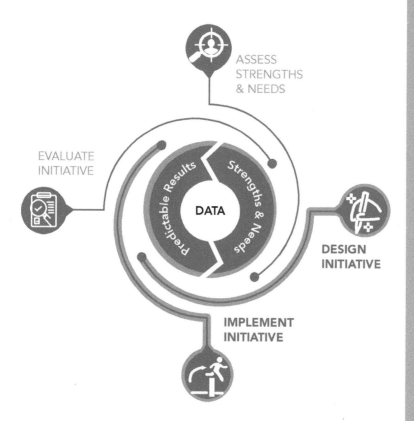

In Part II You Will . . .

- Explore ways to make your initiatives holistic
- Develop your initiative using a range of approaches that include logic modeling
- Define measurable outputs and outcomes to serve as progress touchstones during initiative implementation
- Determine how to situate your initiative within the school or district
- Identify opportunities for early wins to build initiative momentum
- Explore the process of scaling an initiative to increase its impact

 Key Tools

Tool 5: Drawing Conclusions From Your Data

Tool 6: Solutions Based on Barriers and Strengths

Tool 7: Logic Model Building Tool

Tool 8: Defining Fidelity

Tool 9: Partner Readiness Checklist

Tool 10: Initiative Plan Schematic

Tool 11: Evaluation Plan Sections

Self-Assessment: Initiative Design

Use this quick self-assessment to help you determine your prior knowledge for topics covered in Part II: Designing and Launching the Initiative.

HOW MUCH DO YOU KNOW ABOUT	A LOT	A LITTLE	NOT AT ALL	UNSURE
• Logic model components	O	O	O	O
• The concept of fidelity	O	O	O	O
• Embedding an initiative in a school or district's current work and culture	O	O	O	O
• Planning for early wins	O	O	O	O
• Scaling initiatives	O	O	O	O

Designing the Initiative 9

I think perhaps the most difficult thing to explain to someone else is how to analyze the data you'll face. You see, every situation yields different types of data. Plus, what that data says cannot be predicted. And then, you must also acknowledge your context is as unique as the data. So, well, the "how" of this defies a prescriptive analysis approach.

Speaking generally, if that data is **quantitative**, we would typically use a program—from Excel to R or SPSS—to provide descriptive and inferential analysis. If the data is **qualitative**, you would read and code for recurring themes and ideas and likely identify divergent perspectives too. This first level of analysis is typically straightforward. It's something you or your team will want to plan for as you determine the different approaches you will employ for gaining the data you need.

This is also a great time to review the steps you've taken to make your program a success:

- Carefully described the primary gap and contributing gaps that impact it
- Reviewed a range of existing data to understand multiple dimensions of the primary gap and began to investigate both barriers and strengths
- Invited everyone involved to share their voices, views, and visions about the challenge or opportunity
- Engaged in data collection, quantitative and/or qualitative, and then analyzed it to create a summary of key findings from surveys, interviews, focus groups, and/or observations

If you've reached this point, it means that you currently have summary data in front of you. Now is the time to take it in and begin to tentatively draw some conclusions about causes and capabilities. I find it useful to do this individually and with the team. By "team," you might bring together your colleagues, and ideally, you'd invite some of the very people your initiative will target. If it's an initiative to grow the instructional prowess of teachers, have some of them in the room. If it targets students, hear from them as well. The purpose here is to present and discuss what you've learned, and by having multiple people present, you'll hasten a diversity of perspectives and interpretations. Tool 5 offers some helpful questions to be used in reviewing the data and working toward defining tentative solutions.

 TOOL 5: DRAWING CONCLUSIONS FROM YOUR DATA

Purpose	Review both existing and recently collected data in summary form to consider findings, share perspectives on learnings to date, and then explore solutions.
Task	Use this tool to frame the team's review of available data and work toward shared understanding and tentative solutions.

QUESTIONS ABOUT THE DATA

- Looking across the available data, does it make sense? Is it conceivable this data truly represents the people you need to involve in this initiative?
- What evidence do we have that could confirm these findings accurately reflect the involved people(s) and their experiences?
- Where do the visions and viewpoints of your players come together? Where are they split?
- Is any critical voice or viewpoint not yet represented in our data?
- Is there a specific data point you wish we had that proved impossible to get?

QUESTIONS TO SUPPORT INTERPRETATION

- What are the three biggest take-aways that remain in your mind following your individual review of our findings?
- What surprised you most?
- What did you expect to see in the findings that didn't appear?
- Think back to your earliest ideas about this situation, the challenge and the causes. In what ways do these findings differ from your earliest assumptions?

QUESTIONS THAT MOVE TOWARD TENTATIVE SOLUTIONS

- Based on our data, is there evidence a program would offer a positive solution to the primary gap?
- What does the team believe to be the most influential causes? What data supports these conclusions?
- What capabilities are already in place, as part of the system, that stand to support our future efforts?
- What primary and supporting program components will be necessary to positively affect the established causes?
- What do we anticipate will get in the way of the solution or solutions we've discussed? What will we do to reduce the change of that influence?

Moving Toward Holistic Initiatives

As you begin to think about tentative solutions, it is helpful to have an idea of the range of elements you may choose to offer for each type of cause. The strengths you've found are also key here. They will round out the **solution system** that leverages strengths in support of efforts to close the gap (see Tool 6). Essentially, they are your initiative! I refer to **holistic initiatives** because successful initiatives attend to each of the barriers in play. While you are developing learning-and-doing work that will undoubtedly target the knowledge and skills area, you are also going to integrate elements of motivation, incentives, and environment—where merited—to produce a complete initiative. In being complete, you move one step closer to predictable results.

TOOL 6: SOLUTIONS BASED ON BARRIERS AND STRENGTHS

Purpose	An inventory of examples aligned to each category of causes/capabilities to guide early thinking around a program solution.
Task	Use this tool to review the causes and capabilities you find. Consider example solutions that may address causes; acknowledge examples of strengths that may already be present and leveraged to support your program.

BARRIER/ STRENGTH	DEFINITION	POSSIBLE SOLUTIONS/STRENGTHS
Knowledge and Skill	You have the necessary information and sufficient opportunity to practice so that you will be successful	• Professional development and training • Coaching • Reference guides, used during performance • Practice
MOTIVATION	**VALUE × CONFIDENCE = MOTIVATION**	
Value	How much you care about performing	• Hearing how and why others value performance • Connect performance to real-world application • Connect performance to personal goals and aspirations

(Continued)

(Continued)

MOTIVATION	VALUE × CONFIDENCE = MOTIVATION	
Confidence	Your beliefs about whether you will or won't be successful	• Early opportunities for success • Protected opportunities for no- or low-risk practice, with feedback • Seeing the success of others who are perceived to have similar baseline abilities, while avoiding comparison of the gap between • "Chunked" application—experiencing mastery of smaller, sequenced tasks that, together, comprise the larger performance • Goal setting and self-tracking of emerging performance to see mastery grow, self-gathering evidence of success
Incentives	Things the organization offers that reward successful performance	• Favorable organizational climate that recognizes and rewards performance • Taking time to notice performance • Balanced feedback and consequences for performance—success and growth-oriented feedback • Monetary or monetized rewards • Further opportunities—for growth, for leadership
ENVIRONMENT	COMPRISING TOOLS, EXPECTATIONS, AND TIME	
Tools	Ready access to the tools and resources required for successful performance	• Ready access to necessary technologies and program materials • All resources necessary for performance readily available • Reference guides to guide or enlighten performance while it occurs
Expectations	Clear expectations, sometimes through policy, that align with successful performance	• Directives that prioritize performance • Policy that doesn't contradict performance

ENVIRONMENT	COMPRISING TOOLS, EXPECTATIONS, AND TIME	
Time	Established priority for performance that considers the time commitment necessary and accommodates accordingly	<ul><li>Set aside time for performance to reasonably occur</li><li>Clarity around what time allotment performance will replace, in cases where there is no more time in the day</li><li>Integration of efficiencies, to reduce time-to-performance and the time it takes to perform</li></ul>

Your Solution 10

Leading Initiative Design

This is a natural transition point, where you move from listening and contemplating, to documenting our early ideas about the initiative—what's involved, how it will operate, and what we expect to achieve. It is helpful at this stage to be explicit in your thinking.

Remember that design is an iterative process. Your early ideas and plans will change at many points. They'll change before you ever do anything, simply because of your continued thinking and reflection on the needs and the design. Successful initiatives also change during implementation. While our early investigatory efforts will deeply inform the program design, there's no *fully* predicting what will happen when "program meets world." Acknowledge and embrace this truism by building in feedback loops and regular opportunities to intentionally adjust and hone the initiative's initial design. Part of the planning involves baking in such opportunities and a willingness to act upon what you learn.

Introducing the Logic Model

One tool that proves helpful in early program design is the logic model. Maybe you've heard of this planning and elaboration tool? I've sat in funded-program orientation sessions where program officers "trained" the group on logic models. I watched as eyes glazed over, brains seemed to shut down, and people quickly appeared to tune out. My own real-time analysis of this situation suggested two things: Early over-complexification of what a logic model is and does, coupled with and directly causing a huge confidence deficit across most everyone present. (Side note: Did you catch the *cause* analysis I just accomplished there?) Logic models can be incredibly helpful, and they don't need to be complex—at least conceptually.

Logic models, at their most basic level, are composed of three elements:

- What you need—to run the initiative
- What you're going to do—and how you'll know it happened
- What we expect to happen once we do it—and how we'll know we have been successful

If you're familiar with logic models, you'd recognize those three things as inputs, processes, and outcomes. A logic model defines what your program will have, do, and accomplish. In practice, you'll frequently see the second and third categories further broken down. For example, outcomes may be presented in short- and long-term categories. That type of approach is helpful, especially when the ultimate outcome is significant change over time. Examples of that type of situation include raising test scores, operating high functioning professional learning communities, transitioning to a new literacy curriculum across the district. Outcomes like these require definition of short-term outcomes or even short- and intermediate-term outcomes, which quantify the path to success in tangible terms. As you've probably gathered, that path to success is important. Then there is no track; you'll never know if you're on it or off it. You can end up, well, anywhere!

Logic models are organized in various ways across these three categories. For example, the processes might be broken down to include phases that define both program activities and outputs separately. Or a logic model might differentiate between short- and long-term outcomes. In fact, some logic models add mid-term program outcomes. The accompanying figures offer simple and complex examples of logic models.

At the core, a logic model is a tool used to document the initiative's operation and outcomes . . . essentially, its approach to change. That includes defining the resources the program involves, the ways those resources will be used, and the impact the combining of resources and actions is intended to have. Figures 10.1, 10.2, and 10.3 provide three examples of basic logic models.

Figure 10.1 Basic Logic Model for Technology Initiative

the art and science of personalized professional development

INPUTS

What we invest

Human Capital
- Teacher leaders
- Administration
- Support staff
- Central office teams
- Curriculum leaders
- Academic coaches
- Technology experts to integrate systems
- Network partners

Staff Time
- To develop, manage, train on, and adapt PD system

Funding
- To sustain PD system

Technology
- Hardware & software
- District infrastructure
- Interoperable network
- myPD system
- Canvas integration

Shared Teaching & Learning Framework
- California Standards for the Teaching Profession
- Administrator Evaluation Domains & Dimensions

PROCESSES

Activities — What we do

myPD Team conducts differentiated training sessions to build capacity to use myPD:
- Access learning opportunities
- Register for professional development
- Conduct self-assessments
- Find and select aligned learning opportunities
- Reflect on impact of PD on teacher practice and student outcomes

Curriculum staff creates face-to-face and self-paced learning opportunities aligned to district priorities based on needs assessment data, teacher interviews, and observations from the field and gathers feedback on impact

New teachers engage in self-initiated or coach-facilitated cycles of professional learning using myPD

Teachers and administrators access evaluation tools aligned to Teaching & Learning Framework performance indicators within myPD

myPD Team embeds locally developed social media and podcast content in interface to provide multimodal learning experiences

Outputs — Evidence

Teachers use myPD at least once per month to access core curriculum documents and professional learning opportunities (face-to-face and self-paced)

250,000 total logins annually with average 2,500 unique users per month

Staff can access at least 1,000 different self-paced learning opportunities anytime, anywhere via myPD

Induction candidates use myPD to conduct self-assessments, develop their Individualized Learning Plans, access aligned PD, and reflect on the impact of the PD on their practice

Teachers, who opt into evaluation cycles through myPD, set goals and receive feedback aligned to CSTP performance indicators

All certificated management evaluations are conducted in myPD, including self-assessment, goal setting, leadership observations, mid and end-of-year reflections, and final ratings

myPD Unplugged podcast live and myPD Twitter feed embedded within myPD for ease of access

OUTCOMES

Mid Term — Leading Indicators

50% of teachers and administrators access district aligned professional development through myPD at least once per quarter

Self-paced and self-selected learning opportunities available through myPD maintain an average rating of 4 out of 5 stars, when rated by users

Teacher satisfaction with quality of professional development experiences averages 75% Agree or Strongly Agree in all categories assessed

50% of administrators use Year-at-a-Glance docs embedded in myPD to conduct classroom observations

50% of teachers opt into conducting their evaluation in myPD

75% of teacher PD transcripts reflect an average of at least 20 hours of self-selected ongoing learning annually

50% of Year 1 & 50% of Year 2 induction candidates show growth in at least 1 CSTPs over the course of one year

Tweets average 2000 impressions and 200 total engagements to demonstrate teacher/administrator interest in the content

myPD Unplugged podcast live with at least 20,000 streams annually

Long Term — Lagging Indicators

50% of teachers and administrators, who access district aligned professional development through myPD, complete at least one learning opportunity per month

At least 85% of teachers who access, register, or engage in PD via myPD agree or strongly agree that their learning aligned to intended outcomes as reported on exit surveys

75% of administrator classroom walkthroughs and observations of teacher practice demonstrate implementation of CCSS-aligned strategies in core curriculum documents

At least 90% of teachers are effective in all California Standards for the Teaching Profession (CSTP) at the end of an evaluation cycle in myPD

Top 1% of myPD users (teachers) earn a Distinguished for CSTP 6 (Developing as Professional Educator) rating on their final evaluations

50% of Year 1 & 75% of Year 2 induction candidates show growth in at least 2 CSTPs over the course of one year

At least 80% of staff who engage in podcast or social media-based PD report that the content and supporting activities Sufficiently or Substantially informed changes to their practice one month after the learning event

Assumptions

- Anchored in Adult Learning Theory
- Aligned to LBUSD Strategic Plan
- Building on Effective Face-to-Face PD Model
- Complements Technology Infrastructure
- Sustainable Funding
- Common Core State Standards (CCSS)

Situation

Given a well-calibrated, needs-driven professional development system aligned to district priorities, teachers will engage in a learning cycle that uses formative assessments to become more astute, thoughtful, & responsive to student needs as measured by performance evaluations.

Source: Nader Imad Twal

Figure 10.2   Example Logic Model for Home Visit Program

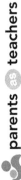 parents as teachers

Evidence-Based Home Visiting Logic Model

GUIDING THEORETICAL FRAMEWORK

Human Ecology and Family Systems | Tenets of Child Development | Developmental Parenting | Attribution Theory | Empowerment and Self-Efficacy

INPUTS

- Implementing agency leadership and support
- Qualified supervisors and parent educators trained in Foundational and Model Implementation
- Participants (families with children ranging from prenatal to kindergarten)
- Technology (database, phones, etc.)
- Sustainable funding
- Policies, procedures and protocols
- Community support and partnerships
- The Foundational curricula, Model Implementation and Supervisor's Handbook
- Comprehensive Affiliate Plan with design elements that meet Parents as Teachers Essential Requirements and Quality Standards
- Program management, evaluation and Continuous Quality Improvement (CQI)
- Implementation, advocacy, data collection and management resources with support from state and national offices

ACTIVITIES

- Reflective Supervision and Professional Development
- Personal Visits
- Group Connections
- Child Screening
- Resource Network
- Family-Centered Assessment and Goal Setting
- Stakeholder Engagement
- Evaluation and Continuous Quality Improvement

OUTPUTS

- Staff receive regular reflective supervision and participate in professional development.
- Families have regular personal visits that include the areas of emphasis and follow the Foundational curricula.
- Group connections are provided for families.
- Children receive regular developmental screening and a health review, including hearing and vision.
- Families are connected to needed community resources.
- Parent educators complete family-centered assessment and support families to set goals.
- Advisory committee meetings are held regularly and advocacy work is conducted.
- Measurement of outcomes and participant satisfaction and participation in the Quality Endorsement and Improvement process.

OUTCOMES

Short-term

- Increased healthy pregnancies and improved birth outcomes.
- Increased early identification and referral to services for possible developmental delays and vision, hearing and health issues in children.
- Increased parent knowledge of age-appropriate child development, including language, cognitive, social-emotional and motor domains.
- Improved parenting capacity, parenting practices and parent-child relationships through the demonstration of positive parenting skills and quality parent-child interactions.
- Improved family health and functioning as demonstrated by a quality home environment, social connections and empowerment.

Intermediate

- Improved child health and development.
- Reduced rates of child abuse and neglect.
- Increased school readiness.
- Increased parent involvement in children's care and education.

Long-term

- Strong communities, thriving families and healthy, safe children who are ready to learn.

—— **Approach: Partner, Facilitate, Reflect**

Vision	Mission	Core Values	Approach

Source: Parents as Teachers

Figure 10.3 Example Logic Model for School Health Program (Partial)

Promoting Adolescent Health Through School-Based HIV/STD Prevention and School-Based Surveillance: FOA PS13-1308 Logic Model

Program Goals: Reduce HIV and other STD infections among adolescents; and

Reduce disparities in HIV infections and other STD experienced by specific adolescent sub-populations.

INPUTS	STRATEGIES & WORK PLAN REQUIREMENTS	SHORT-TERM OUTCOMES	INTERMEDIATE OUTCOMES	5-YEAR OUTCOMES
Funding • CDC/DASH • Leveraged funds and resources **Administrative** • 100% qualified FTE to manage program • HIV Review Panel • Program monitoring • 5-year strategic plan and annual plans **CDC Resources** • Data on health risk behaviors and school policies and practices • Guidelines, Health Education Curriculum Assessment Tool, School Health Index, and other tools **Partnerships** • CDC/DASH • MOU/MOA with health agencies and health care providers	**Strategy 1: School-Based Surveillance (SURV)** • Collect, analyze, and disseminate scientifically valid data on adolescent health risk behaviors, including sexual risk behaviors, using the Youth Risk Behavior Survey (YRBS); and on school health policies and practices, including sexual health policies and practices, using the School Health Profiles (Profiles) **Strtegy 2: School-Based HIV/STD Prevention (SB)** Approach A: Exemplary Sexual Health Education (ESHE)* • Establish a written MS/HS standard course of study or curriculum framework that reflects ESHE • Develop and foster the use of a systematic process for identifying, selecting or adapting, and implementing ESHE curricula • Establish and maintain a technical assistance and professional development system to assist districts and school in implementing ESHE Approach B: Key Sexual Health Services (SHS)† • Educate school staff and decision makers about the importance of key sexual health services for adolescents • Build the capacity of school staff to deliver or help students access key SHS • Facilitate the provision of SHS through school health services/nursing staff, school-based health centers (SBHC), or visiting staff from public health agencies or health care centers • Establish a referral system with partner organizations that have an expertise in adolescent SHS • Provide guidance to districts and schools on how to increase reimbursement for eligible services	**SURV** All funded sites have weighted YRBS data and weighted Profiles data Approach A: ESHE • Increased number of schools that implement ESHE • Increased number of students in grades 7-12 who receive education to prevent HIV and other STD Approach B: SHS Increased number of schools that: • Establish linkages with organizations that have an expertise in adolescent SHS • Establish a system to refer students to youth-friendly providers for key SHS	Increased student knowledge and skills to prevent HIV/STD and pregnancy Improved student attitudes and norms in support of HIV/STD and pregnancy prevention Improved student access to youth-friendly key SHS delivered Improved students safety at school Improved students connectedness to school and supportive adults	Decreased % of adolescents Who: • Have ever had sexual intercourse • Are currently sexually active • Have had sexual intercourse with four or more persons in their lifetime Increased % of sexually active adolescents who: • Use condoms • Use both condoms and hormonal contraception methods

(Continued)

(Continued)

INPUTS	STRATEGIES & WORK PLAN REQUIREMENTS	SHORT-TERM OUTCOMES	INTERMEDIATE OUTCOMES	5-YEAR OUTCOMES
• Federal agencies (e.g., OAH, ACF) • CDC-funded programs (e.g., DHAP, DSTDP, DVH, NCIRD, DRH) • DASH-funded SEA, TEA, LEA, and NGO • NGO/CBO • SBHC or SLHC • School nurses • Hospitals/health care providers • Sexual health and teen pregnancy prevention coalitions • Consultants	Approach C: Safe and Supportive Environments for Students and Staff (SSE) • Implement policies and procedures to prevent bullying and sexual harassment on school property and off-campus at school-sponsored events • Implement policies and practices to prevent electronic aggression (e.g., cyber-bullying and sexting) • Implement and enforce policies and procedures that increase school connectedness and parent engagement • Establish student-led clubs and program activities that promote a positive school environment • Create opportunities for students to participate in mentoring and service learning programs with teachers and other adults Approach D: Educate Decision Makers on Policy; Implement and Track Policy (Policy)‡ • Assess and identify gaps in, and track implementation of, current state and local policies related to school-based HIV/STD prevention • Educate decision makers and stakeholders on potential policy solutions to address school health issues related to HIV/STD prevention • Provide technical assistance on implementing current school health policies related to HIV/STD prevention • Establish and maintain state and district-level School Health Advisory Councils (SHAC) • Promote the use of the School Health Index	• Provider on-site key SHS • Receive reimbursement for eligible services provided on-site <u>Approach C: SSE</u> Increased number of schools that: • Prohibit bullying and sexual karassment • Improve parent engagement • Promote school connectedness <u>Approach D: POLICY</u> • Increased number of states and districts that track policy implementation and educate decision makers on policy solutions • Increased number of schools using the School Health Index	Improved student: • Attendance at school • Academic achievement	• Have been tested for HIV and received treatments after testing positive • Have been tested for STD and received treatment after testing positive • Have been tested for pregnancy Increased % of adolescents who are fully immunized for HPV

INPUTS	STRATEGIES & WORK PLAN REQUIREMENTS	SHORT-TERM OUTCOMES	INTERMEDIATE OUTCOMES	5-YEAR OUTCOMES
	Strategy 3: Capacity Building Assistance for School-Based HIV/STD Prevention (CBA) • Modify, as needed, existing tools, resources, and materials and train SEA/TEA/LEA staff to implement them • Provide capacity building assistance to SEA/TEA/LEA staff necessary to implement their required FOA strategies • Develop strategic partnerships and collaborations between SEA/TEA/LEA and members/chapters/affiliates/other organizations to support implementation			

Source: Centers for Disease Control

*Exemplary Sexual Health Education (ESHE): A systematic, evidence-informed approach to sexual health education that includes the use of grade-specific, evidence-based interventions (EBI), but also emphasizes sequential learning across elementary, middle, and high school grade levels. ESHE provides adolescents the essential knowledge and critical skills needed to avoid HIV infection, other STD, and unintended pregnancy. ESHE is delivered by well-qualified and trained teachers, uses strategies that are relevant and engaging, and consists of elements that are medically accurate, developmentally and culturally appropriate, and consistent with the scientific research on effective sexual health education. For more information: www.cdc.gov/healthyyouth/sher/characteristics/index.htm and www.cdc.gov/healthyyouth/hecat/pdf/HECAT_Module_SH.pdf.

†Key Sexual Health Services (SHS) include, for the purpose of this FOA, anticipatory guidance for prevention including delaying the onset of sexual activity; promoting HIV and STD testing, counselling, and treatment, and the dual use of condoms and highly effective contraceptives among sexually active adolescents; HIV and STD testing, counselling, and referral; pregnancy testing; and HPV vaccinations.

‡Policies, including laws, regulations, procedures, administrative actions, incentives, or voluntary practices of governments and other institutions, that can impact the delivery of exemplary sexual health education, referral to key sexual health services, and establishment of safe and supportive school environments for students and staff.

TOOL 7: LOGIC MODEL BUILDING TOOL

Purpose	Produce a logic model to represent the program you will be evaluating.
Task	Use this tool and its guidance to identify inputs, processes, and outcomes for the targeted program. Make sure to ask leadership and the program developer if a logic model already exists.

INPUTS	IMPLEMENTATION		OUTCOMES	
	PROCESSES	OUTPUTS	SHORT-TERM	LONG-TERM/ IMPACT
YOUR PLANNED WORK			YOUR INTENDED RESULTS	
Guidance: Inputs describe the resources that will be directed toward the initiative. You might also think about inputs as the "investments" made into the initiative. Consider human, financial, and organizational resources.	Processes are the things that will be accomplished to implement the initiative. Processes describe how the initiative will use the inputs (resources). Consider the intentional program activities— including tools, training, and events that, together, are designed to bring about the outcomes.	Processes lead to outputs. Outputs are metrics by which we can assess the initiative's implementation progress, including implementation fidelity.	Short-term outcomes, sometimes referenced as "outputs" typically describe accomplishment of the defined processes. Consider what might provide the earliest evidence that the program is having even the most limited impact. Short-term outcomes are typically those things that point to "promising results," which lead to longer-term impact.	Long-term outcomes stem from the goals of the initiative and the needs the initiative was intended to address. These outcomes should describe positive change for the people your initiative will reach. Consider growth in knowledge or skills, positive changes in attitudes or confidence levels (self-efficacy), and desired changes for your participants' actions (performance).

INPUTS	IMPLEMENTATION		OUTCOMES	
	PROCESSES	OUTPUTS	SHORT-TERM	LONG-TERM/ IMPACT
YOUR PLANNED WORK			YOUR INTENDED RESULTS	

Having taken a look at a few logic models, let me highlight why I believe they are a necessary part of any initiative's design and implementation.

First, they define the initiative's details and how those details are intended to turn into results, or outcomes. I've mentioned before that, as a **program evaluator**, I'm often retained to document a program's implementation and impact. When I'm called to evaluate a program where details haven't been fully specified, I find myself building a logic model simply to help me and the person leading the initiative to efficiently define, or fill in, program details—all so I know what to measure! It's incredible that many programs exist today without such definition.

Additionally, logic models can help to ensure you, the people asking for the initiative, the people supporting the initiative, and the people who will participate in the initiative are on the same page when it comes to how the program operates (or will operate). As you sketch your early ideas about the initiative, its elements, and its intended impact, the logic model is a visual you can share with interested allies. It offers an at-a-glance picture and provides something to which people can immediately react.

Finally, the logic model's definition provides a helpful direction you can hand over to an evaluator when someone external will be evaluating and determining the impact of your initiative. As an evaluator myself, when I come in to evaluate something with a logic model, I'm thrilled! A successful logic model succinctly points me to both process and outcome measures to pursue. As evaluator, I can hit the ground running when things are spelled out with a logic model—rather than working to make my own sense of the initiative and its impact. Unfortunately, in such cases, more times than not, there is no logic model available.

Defining Outputs and Outcomes

One of the most important elements of the logic model comes in defining the tangibles the initiative will produce. You'll recognize them in our Logic Model Building Tool (Tool 7) as the outputs and the outcomes.

Outputs describe observable and measurable elements of successful implementation. They answer the question, "What evidence do we have that we're implementing the program the way it was designed?"

Outcomes are the observable and measurable results that come from successful program operation. They answer the question, "What do we expect to happen for the people involved in the initiative when we're successful?"

So outputs tell us we're on the right track and we're doing the things the initiative requires. In essence, they measure whether the implementation is on track. Outcomes identify what the initiative, when successful, will bring about for the people who participate and our organization at large.

TALES FROM THE FIELD: "YOU'VE ALWAYS HAD THE POWER"

So one of my favorite quotes comes from the movie, *The Wizard of Oz*. It's Glinda the Good Witch who offers that encouragement as she helps Dorothy to make good use of the skills, abilities, and powers she has always possessed.

I'm often reminded of that quote when classroom educators turn into program planners and staff developers. Here, I so often see amazing educators of all kinds—elementary, middle, high, special education, English learner experts—seemingly forget so many of the things that make them amazing as they assume a role leading programs.

This most often manifests itself with outcomes. Most every one of these educators had demonstrated the ability to understand—even unpack—standards and successfully teach to them in their classrooms and to students of all levels. And yet, when faced with planning an initiative that requires them to plan for the teaching of new knowledge and skills to adults, including their peers, that outcomes focus often flies out the window.

Instead of defining clear, measurable outcomes and then defining a systematic initiative to achieve them, the work so often begins with, "Who can we get to come be a speaker?" Or, "Wouldn't it be great if we could take them to XYZ conference?"

I've joked in the past that when we're limiting our initiative planning to events, we're basically planning parties, not initiatives.

As educators, we are well-acquainted with objectives and outcomes. So if you're someone who is moving to defining outcomes for your peers, I want to encourage you to use that expertise. Outcomes are outcomes—and they work really well for both young people and adults. Channel this superpower you've always had and watch how well-defined outcomes make the difference in focusing the next initiative you design.

What's Measured Matters

You might have noticed my use of the words "observable and measurable" more than once. They're quite important. You see, what's measured matters.

People often speak in broad, casually defined terms: "Student achievement will rise," "We'll achieve equity in hiring," "Transformative leadership will result." Each is a noble pursuit, and yet—what does each one really mean? How will you know it when we see it?

Some time ago, Mager (1997) referred to such broad statements of intent as **fuzzies.** People like fuzzies; they keep us in a position where we aren't fully committing. Hiding behind a fuzzy leaves room—usually *lots* of room—to demonstrate any version of "success." If any outcome will do, then a fuzzy might serve you well. The problem is that we've uncovered specific and compelling needs. For that very reason, *any* outcome will absolutely *not* do.

As you work to define both outputs and outcomes, phrase them in observable and measurable terms. How will you know you've been successful? I would suggest they should be concrete to the point where two people, observing the same evidence, would make the same conclusion about whether they were or were not achieved.

Part III's section titled *Developing Evaluation Questions* offers additional guidance about this very topic. You'll come to find that our evaluation questions, which are based on the outputs and outcomes defined in this current stage, must also be fully observable and measurable. For more support in defining successful outcomes, I recommend a "pre-screening" of this section.

Road Map and Place Mat

I like to think of the logic model as both road map and place mat. As a road map, it defines inputs, processes, and outcomes; it offers a tangible list of what the program will involve and how you will know you've been successful.

But you should also use the current version of your logic model as a place mat. Bring it to every meeting and conversation. Place a copy in front of each participant. This almost literally keeps everyone on the same page as you discuss the emerging ideas and components and work to hone the initiative's design through discussion, consultation, and reflection.

Your place mat will also prove helpful during implementation, as you share the initiative with your team and perhaps train those who will lead various elements. There is only good to come from a shared understanding of the initiative and the *logic* behind its design. When people, together, see it summarized on the page, it provides something to react to and something to consider as the emergent program is pictured, considered, and taken closer to perfection by identifying missing elements or necessary modifications.

Facts About Fidelity 11

If you've been around programs in schools for any amount of time, the word **fidelity** has undoubtedly come up in conversation. Fidelity describes how close an initiative's implementation matches its design. For example, if you were implementing an online program designed to increase reading ability, you might stipulate various fidelity dimensions like frequency of use, modules attempted and completed over time, or even the integration of the online program into each teacher's existing instructional plans.

I've stressed that your planning effort is necessary for several reasons. But chief among them is designing something that yields predictable results. Fidelity is a critical element of your initiative plan. In the absence of fidelity-defined implementation expectations, any type and amount of implementation becomes acceptable.

So what fidelity measures should you use? The answer to that question rests in the needs assessment data you've gathered, an understanding of the people who will be implementing the initiative, the people who will be participating in your initiative, and outcomes you want to reach.

While the specific fidelity details are as unique as the initiative itself, there are some common categories into which fidelity descriptions fall. The following five dimensions (Tool 8) are frequently cited in the program design and evaluation literature (for example, Dusenbury et al., 2003; Mihalic, 2004). They provide some helpful touchstones as you contemplate your program's design and establish expectations for its implementation.

In defining fidelity, not only are you providing a benchmark for those who will implement the program, but you're also contributing to the evaluation of your program by setting the metrics by which successful implementation will be determined. You do yourself and your program a favor by getting this specific early on rather than leaving it to those doing the implementation to simply "figure out" down the line. Use the following tool to think through key fidelity elements. Attention to each category will help you refine and add detail to your program's design.

TOOL 8: DEFINING FIDELITY

SECTION	OUR PLAN
Purpose	Define the specifics that will be used to determine fidelity of initiative implementation: What evidence will we use to confirm the initiative was delivered as designed?
Task	Use this tool to discuss and then define each dimension of fidelity for your envisioned initiative.
SECTION	**OUR PLAN**
Expectations—specific to the content, frequency, duration, and coverage of the initiative's implementation	
Exposure/Dose—of initiative in which participants are required to engage to benefit (establish dosage boundaries to define successful participation)	
Quality of Implementation—of initiative implementation (e.g., quality of leadership, program oversight, coaching, teaching, etc.)	
Reactions of People Involved—how we intend to ensure our teachers and students—or whomever the initiative engages—find relevance in their participation	
Initiative Differentiation—how we intend to make certain our initiative is unique and different from others that may address similar outcomes	

Mapping the Initiative to Your School or District   12

People generally agree that when initiatives are carefully embedded in an organization, they have more of a chance of being successful. As you continue forward and begin to contemplate your initiative solution in response to identified needs, it is also time to think about how it will "attach" to your organization.

Successfully "attached" initiatives have a greater chance of predictable results, especially when compared to those that seem like "something extra." As you've seen, there are many things that threaten even the best initiative's success and impact when they reach the implementation stage. Lack of time, low priority, and failing to clearly articulate the program's alignment to the organization and its needs all stand in the way of streamlining success.

But picture the opposite. Picture an initiative that naturally resides within a school or district. It's been carefully crafted to address specific needs. The implementation is intentional because it is integrated into at least some of the efforts already happening. Making it a district priority makes good sense, because this new initiative aligns with current priorities in the school or district.

Compare that to the opposite sort of "orphan" implementation. I sometimes call this the **"B-52" model of initiative implementation.** A plane flies over your school, drops the initiative off, and heads on out to the next stop. The initiative hits the ground and its success is largely determined by chance. Will someone take an interest in running it? Will anyone note how and where it matches or complements the current efforts? Who will make sense of this newcomer? History has suggested that B-52 implementation is rarely successful. Even worse, the initiative never receives the chance to demonstrate the positive outcomes it might bring to bear on the people it targets.

Creating initiatives that match both needs *and* organizations and bolstering their success by attaching to work already in place just makes sense. How you go about doing that, however, does depend on whether you're implementing an existing initiative or building one of your own and fully from the ground up.

Off-the-Shelf

Off-the-shelf programs and initiatives are prepackaged. Some are purchased, while others could be free and, perhaps, produced by a nonprofit or governmental agency. For example, many nonprofit groups have developed curricula that are used in schools every day. The extent to which they are developed does vary. So that's something to assess as you investigate a proposed program and determine its "fit" to your needs and organization.

I often compare attaching someone else's product to your school or district's work to getting an organ transplant. The chances of success are necessarily limited when we just grab the first lung available and quickly stitch it in. So too with initiatives.

They should directly address identified needs. Likewise, requirements for their implementation and operation should play to capabilities identified in your needs assessment. In the event you identify a high-potential initiative, it's critical to check for compatibility with identified needs and with organizational capabilities.

Ask yourself whether a potential initiative can readily integrate into your organization and be sustained over time and to the point of impact. Implementing an initiative that isn't well matched will certainly be an uphill battle. Doing the compatibility check guards against finding yourself in a suboptimal situation where implementation must be fought at every stage.

Growing Your Own

It can be a challenge to find an initiative with the right fit. That is why, after searching at length, folks sometimes choose to make their own from scratch.

This category consists of initiatives that are fully dreamed, developed, and managed by you or you and your team. This is the "starting from scratch" category, and it usually results from a need and a desire to address that need. Maybe you've looked around for an off-the-shelf solution and found nothing that fits. In fact, if you have done that, great. It shows that you are already weighing needs and considering how likely any given initiative will succeed in your unique setting. Embedding a homegrown initiative in the organization may actually be easier, compared to the off-the-shelf option. For the very reason that their design and implementation are fully under your control, these initiatives should vividly reflect your organization's needs and play to its strengths. As you design the initiative, it's important to regularly reflect back on the needs you seek to address. Likewise, knowing your strengths and leveraging them as strongholds in the design will further ensure your initiative's implementation and success. Such efforts accelerate the time to full implementation and can create an early success, which can help fuel the implementation over time.

Benefitting From Partnerships

Sometimes there isn't an off-the-shelf solution that meets your needs, and you don't have the capacity to build one from scratch. When this situation presents itself, one attractive solution is a partnership.

Partnerships have much to recommend. When developed with care and commitment, the whole can become greater than the sum of its parts. However, partnerships require considerable investments of time and resources to not only be successful but to simply operate as a coordinated whole.

The art of partnering goes beyond the scope of this initiative-focused book. However, in the spirit of exploring as well as ensuring successful partnerships, I do want to offer interested leaders some key points to consider. Tool 9 will guide you through a range of considerations to entertain as you contemplate whether you're ready to partner.

TOOL 9: PARTNER READINESS CHECKLIST

Purpose	Guide early review of an opportunity that could benefit from a partnership.
Task	Use this tool as a checklist to guide your reflection on your readiness for partnering.

DESCRIPTION AND GUIDANCE

- I believe collaboration can benefit addressing identified needs.

- I have identified and assessed community needs and have chosen to pursue a need that may be better met through collaboration.

- I have realistic expectations about what program-based collaboration will require.

- I am aware of potential partnership challenges, such as overcoming cultural differences and philosophies between our organizations.

- I have identified the contributions our organization can bring to a partnership and the constraints we face and intend to address through a partnership.

- I have identified a shortlist of partners with whom I am comfortable engaging in collaboration.

- I have a basic understanding of the prospective partners' organizations and cultures, and I believe that we can collaborate effectively.

- I feel that my partner's goals are aligned with mine and that our assets complement each other and match the community need.

DID YOU KNOW? POWERFUL PARTNERSHIPS

A broad range of factors underlie successful community partnerships. They include the general areas of group cohesion (Barnes et al., 2009), partner participation (Granner & Sharpe, 2004), and partnership simplicity (Martin et al., 2005). Diving a bit deeper, six of the most cited categories into which indicators of successful partnerships can be placed are presented in the Table 12.1.

Table 12.1   Community Partnerships Success Criteria

CATEGORY	SUCCESS CRITERIA
Shared Mission and Values	Stakeholders have a clear understanding of each other's vision and values with a mutual commitment to shared goals, in the most successful partnerships (Nolan, 2011). The Education Development Center (2014) suggests that the "articulated mission and shared beliefs exist and serve as guides for the work of the partnership" (p. 9).
Well-Defined Goals and Objectives	Springing forth from the mission and vision, goals and objectives provide the next level of detail in the pursuit of defining the partnership's work. Make them clear, measurable, openly shared, and monitored throughout the duration of the partnership (Education Development Center, 2014).
Conducive Organizational Structure	Successful partnerships establish a structure that reflects the mission and goals of the collaborative arrangement. It can take the form of an affiliation agreement, legal entity, memorandum of understanding (MOU), or other less formal arrangements, such as a community coalition (Commonwealth Center for Governance Studies, Inc, 2014).
Effective Communication	Communication binds the partnership's ongoing work together. The Commonwealth Center for Governance Studies, Inc (2014), defined effective communication as a system of communication channels among partners, staff, the community, and other stakeholders, which are clear and transparent. Nolan (2011) notes success comes from communication among members, which is straightforward and based on trust and clear, simple reporting.
Synergy	Lasker et al. (2001) defined synergy as the extent to which the perspectives, resources, and skills of the participating individuals and organizations contribute to and strengthen the work of the partnership. Synergy is related to trust and has been defined using concepts such as reliability, sharing a common mission, and willingness to engage in an open conversation (Robert Wood Johnson Foundation, 2009).

(Continued)

(Continued)

CATEGORY	SUCCESS CRITERIA
Shared Resources, Power, and Ownership	Shared resources, power, and decision-making are key to successful partnerships. These shared resources needed to reach objectives can be hard—for example, money, space, equipment, goods such as technology—and soft—for example, information, endorsements, networking connections, skills, and expertise (Brinkerhoff, 2002; Lasker et al., 2001).

The Initiative Plan 13

Here's some good news: You've already been building your initiative plan little-by-little. You have your needs assessment data that justifies the need for the initiative. You also have your drafted logic model that offers an efficient view into what the initiative will involve, how it will operate, and the outcomes it is designed to return.

The **initiative plan** summarizes all of this helpful information. In it, you will supplement that information with some additional details to provide readers with a complete understanding of what you've designed.

Each initiative is unique. Your context will drive your plan's content and how elaborate the plan must be. A local initiative limited to your school site might require a less detailed project plan; a districtwide initiative or grant-funded effort will typically require more. Tool 10 will guide your project plan development and support you as you consider the full range of information a plan could include.

TOOL 10: INITIATIVE PLAN SCHEMATIC	
TYPICAL INITIATIVE PLAN ELEMENTS TO DEFINE AND DOCUMENT	
Purpose	Summarize common sections of a successful initiative plan.
Task	Use this tool to guide the development of your initiative plan and the sections it will contain.
SECTION	**DESCRIPTION AND GUIDANCE**
Introduction	A short and concise overview of the initiative. This section should also name the organization and people involved.

(Continued)

(Continued)

SECTION	DESCRIPTION AND GUIDANCE
Background	Provides descriptions of the following: Organization: background material about the organization, its mission, and how the initiative relates to the organization's work. People: name those asking for the initiative and briefly describe the full set of people involved as leaders, thought partners, and those who will eventually participate in the initiative.
Needs Assessment Summary	Summarize your needs assessment effort: Outline the different needs assessment tasks you completed Share the summarized data generated by the needs assessment. Offer your conclusions, based on the summarized data, that justifies the initiative you will propose.
Program	A detailed description of the initiative you are proposing: Share and describe the logic model—realizing that many people who read your plan will be unfamiliar with this helpful tool. Describe the various activities your initiative will involve. Connect them to one another and the initiative-at-large rather than limiting your description to a basic list of bulleted activities. Connect the elements to needs assessment data, such that your reader is readily able to picture how the initiative closely aligns with the needs you've documented.
Timeline	Provide a detailed timeline: Share your commitment for development, including the tasks and the timeline on which they will be completed. Carefully consider sequencing by (a) considering the order in which tasks must be completed—in other words, identifying prerequisite tasks; and (b) identifying tasks that can be pursued in parallel, potentially offering efficiency in your initiative development. Assign members of the initiative development team to each task and then comb the timeline to make sure time expectations are reasonable for each task, as well as each team member's allocation. Offer a sample timeline for the initiative's operation. If it is a program that runs annually, produce a one-year timeline that depicts a typical year.
Roles and Responsibilities	The "who" behind your initiative, make sure to describe the following: The personnel who will be involved in the development. Include descriptions of each role and the amount of time you anticipate each role will require. The personnel required for the initiative's operation. Again, define the roles and time allocations.

SECTION	DESCRIPTION AND GUIDANCE
Partnerships	If your initiative is relying on services or individuals outside your organization, it is important to describe these partnerships in the plan. Make the role or roles of partners explicitly clear. Also note who on your team will manage the partnership and who will be the point-of-contact for each partnering organization.
Risks and Mitigation Strategies	A successful plan anticipates what could go wrong and has a plan to deal with such "risks" before they even happen. Take some time to brainstorm with your team and define the various barriers you might encounter, the "what ifs" that are on the minds of team members, and any other unwelcome developments that could befall your initiative's success. Then, decide what you would do in each situation. Successful leaders constantly guard against risks and keep them from growing to the point of true threats. Taking some time to anticipate risks at this early juncture will also build your team's collective vigilance as they guard against potential derailments.
Program Monitoring and Evaluation	Later, I'll guide your development of an evaluation plan. At this point, you should spend some time defining how you will monitor the initiative's progress. It is a good idea to also briefly suggest how the logic model-defined outcomes—both short and long term—will be measured and when such measurement data will be collected, analyzed, and reported. Once defined, I would also encourage you to circle back to the timeline and add this commitment to monitoring and reporting at the relevant times.

Launching the Plan

Having a program plan in writing is a significant accomplishment. The needs assessment and logic modeling have paid off and given you the necessary clarity to formulate your initiative and detail its design.

As your thoughts turn to implementing the plan, you will need to pay close attention to a range of things that will directly intersect with your initiative and its success. As you launch the plan, now is a great time to strategize the implementation-boosting practices that I will describe with your team.

Pressing the "White Space"

Many authors have referred to the white space in an organization (Maletz & Nohria, 2001; Rummler et al., 2009). Often, this is within the context of the organization chart (or "org chart," for short). Picturing your own org chart and considering what I've just described, I'm sure you would quickly observe that "getting things done" isn't that simple. One reason is that most of the work happens *between* the boxes on the org chart. That area is called the *white space.*

Recognizing the white space in your organization is critical to getting things done. You've just poured plenty of your expertise, understanding, and intent into an initiative plan. But now, the real work is about to begin as you launch into developing the initiative and then implementing it. Your initiative plan describes the immediate team necessary to build it, along with the other resources on which you'll depend to make the dream a reality.

All that intention coupled with "explicitness" for what you will design and do should be satisfying. But I want you to take an additional, intentional moment to think through the white space in your organization and anticipate what will happen as your initiative plan is put into action.

- Does your initiative plan reflect the "real" way things are done in your organization—or is it dependent on how they "should" be done?

- What unwritten yet codified relationships exist across the white space of your organization that could either support or challenge your work?

- Who has been unintentionally left out of the plan but in time will become a necessary stakeholder in your implementation?

- How will you bring together the varied and diverse people and teams involved in support of your initiative, even those who are tangentially, yet necessarily, involved?

Successful leaders and developers nimbly navigate the white space in their organizations. When you see this, it is as if they defy the hierarchy of the org chart as they establish buy-in and support across a school district.

Acknowledging, anticipating, and advancing the white space will help your initiative efforts succeed. But success in navigating the white space means your efforts will also meet with less pushback and wasted energy.

DID YOU KNOW? DEIMPLEMENTATION

There is absolutely no shortage of initiatives and programs in our daily lives. That's especially true for educators and education leaders who grapple with high expectations and limited hours in their days. Thus, it only makes sense that any new initiative is designed with the recognition of other initiatives that are already in place. In fact, anything that intersects with and could influence the initiative that you're planning should be fully considered.

It is here that I think we educators can learn something from the medical sciences' concept of **deimplementation**. Within the medical context, the term refers to "the process of reducing care that is harmful, ineffective, overused, or not cost-effective" (Wolf et al., 2021, p. 231). Wolf et al. suggest deimplementation in their area of pediatrics happens within four areas. Education thinkers, including DeWitt (2022), have observed the connection between these ideas and the work of educators. Consider how easily the ideas are applied to our own practices with initiatives (see Table 13.1).

Table 13.1 Applying Deimplementation to Initiatives

RECOMMENDATIONS IN PEDIATRIC MEDICINE (WOLF ET AL., 2021, P. 232)	APPLYING DEIMPLEMENTATION RECOMMENDATIONS TO EDUCATION
Developing benchmarks for low-value care for specific conditions so that doctors can be evaluated on their progress	Using defined benchmarks to assess effectiveness of initiatives, programs, and strategies to differentiate low and high value
Measuring the harms of overuse for children	Assessing policies and practices that, when overused, result in negative outcomes for children (e.g., disproportionality in special education referrals)
Understanding the best ways to stop each type of low-value care	Carefully and intentionally planning the deimplementation process using change theory to bring about better states
Considering any potential unintended consequences of deimplementation	Understanding and protecting successful elements of otherwise ineffective or low-value programs

(Continued)

(Continued)

Continuously adding to our practice only results in watered down practice and results. When considered solely from an "available time" perspective, adding without subtraction means less time given to expectation.

The time has come to apply the concept and practice of deimplementation to our work leading effective initiatives that fire across all dimensions of student success. One way to start is by routinely considering existing initiatives within the context of the initiative being planned. What are you already doing—and to what results? Likely, if you're already doing something . . . while, at the same time planning something new . . . there is going to be something worthy of deimplementing. Make initiative planning the time to inventory programs and initiatives that are already in place and give full consideration to which would exist within the "ideal" world.

Program Leadership

This section on the initiative plan has involved quite the discussion of people and organizations. But that's for good reason. You see, without a dedicated leader who knows or can quickly know the organization into which the initiative must enter, things may falter before they even get started.

I remember some good friends sharing the news that they would be welcoming a new member into their family. They had dreamed of that very thing for years, set their intentions, and carefully planned financially and logistically for it to happen. The time spent leading up to the baby's arrival was filled with more planning and preparation. Naturally, that included preparing a room for the baby, as well as care on all fronts—from medical care to near- and farther-term care when they both would go back to work. In sum, they knew their goals, they knew their current lifestyle, they anticipated and accommodated the new lifestyle, and they created the necessary environment for all that to occur. Now, for a quick second, compare that to the couple that ends up expecting, does absolutely nothing, the baby comes, they head home from the hospital, look around and think, "Hmmm . . . we're going to need some stuff."

Of course, it's ridiculous. The second scenario would never happen, I hope. When a life is on the line and when success isn't negotiable, we plan, prepare, facilitate, and adapt.

A new initiative coming into an organization has similar needs. Whether that's recognized or not is another story. The initiative, developed in isolation and then delivered to the doorstep of the organization may—or may not—meet with a positive reception.

Defining Program Leadership

In my mind, there are two distinct leadership roles at play in a program's early stage: the initiative creator and the initiative implementor.

There is the creator who is responsible for the initiative's design and development. This person oversees the needs assessment and design and then leads the initiative's development effort to the point of being ready for implementation.

There is also a necessary leader who oversees and manages the implementation. Let's call them the implementor. This person is responsible for making sure implementation happens with success by eliminating the challenges and roadblocks that inevitably arise and continuously advocates for the initiative across the organization (in other words, making the initiative matter).

Can the same person fulfill both roles? Absolutely! In many cases, especially with smaller efforts, people can and do. However, in other cases, people with deep subject matter expertise oversee the development of a detailed initiative, which is then delivered to another part of the organization, which is responsible for its broad implementation and oversight.

It is likely that your school and district's composition, available resources, and strategic plan will all influence whether design and development and implementation are managed by the same dynamic leader or require different personnel. And yet, regardless of whether you're developing or implementing, the skills and aptitudes that make implementation leaders successful share far more similarities than differences.

Leading Implementation Action Planning

14

Programs, by their very definition, mean change. When born of and matched to needs, programs cause change—through their arrival, implementation, and integration into the organization. Ideally, they produce positive change and bring your school or district to a better state as they address identified needs and impact the people who participate.

Choosing a Program Leader

With all this change, it is critical to have an effective individual overseeing the program from its earliest implementation planning. From what you've read so far, it is no surprise that the ideal is to have the designated individual engaged from the earliest needs assessment efforts. When that cannot happen, the minimum point of entry comes when implementation planning kicks off.

Implementers are, above all else, change agents and change facilitators. They must be skilled communicators, consensus builders, and champions. Let's look at some of the nonnegotiable skills successful implementation managers bring to their roles.

Roles and Responsibilities

Successful program implementations typically have dynamic leaders and champions at their helm. There is no one "right" experience that best qualifies someone to lead a program. However, in my experience evaluating hundreds of programs and underlying success factors, I believe the following are critical attributes when considering program leadership.

Stability

The individual should be selected with attention to anticipated longevity in their role. Turnover impacts implementation and, especially, the ongoing efforts to sustain programs over time.

Cross-Organization View and Connections

The implementation manager should have knowledge of the schools and district in the broadest sense. The role requires someone who knows and can regularly interface with individuals across the organization. A good implementation manager leverages organization strengths, creates symbiotic relationships with other implementation managers, unites leaders in support of their program, and sustains interest and support from all involved over time.

As discussed, this also involves navigating the white space of the organization chart, to both facilitate work in the way it happens (rather than how it is "supposed" to happen) and forge (or mend) necessary relationships where there is no explicit hierarchy to compel collaboration. Said a bit more plainly, implementation managers are often in the position of having the responsibility to get things done, without full, managerial control over the resources they require. Success requires diplomacy, persistence, and the ability to make people want to play, even when they don't have to do so.

Champion

Yes, part of what I've just described is this: the **champion**. The implementation manager must be skilled at advocating for the program and communicating its design, operation, and impact to necessary supporters in the organization—from staff and students, to leadership, parents, and families. Programs that lack true champions regularly suffer short lifespans.

Long-Term Commitment

Speaking of championing the program over time, an implementation manager recently shared with me that, given the opportunity to do their program's implementation all over again, they would be "so much more deliberate about sustainability." This is a common realization that surfaces as programs move from their initial implementation phase into routine operation.

In these cases, it seems that, over time, other matters rivet their attention away from the program they have worked so hard to launch. Then, the often-seen result is an implementation that wanes or falters. I've seen, time again, that the reward for being successful leading one program is getting two or three more to manage!

For each of these reasons, it is critical to make program management a deliberate part of program design. That necessarily includes a realistic amount of dedicated time allocated for the implementation manager to support both the launch and ongoing oversight of the program over time.

Identifying Roles and Responsibilities

I've admitted that when I think implementation manager, I think change agent. But they cannot accomplish this work alone. Effective program plans not only detail how the program will operate, but they define roles and responsibilities for all personnel involved. Now is a great time to pull out that logic model (see Tool 7) and review what "inputs" you have listed in the first column. Likely, personnel are among the necessary resources listed there. Hopefully, these people have been involved in the needs assessment and planning work you've done up until this point. If so, the work of the implementation manager has already involved the consensus and champion work that role requires.

But now is the time to document roles, responsibilities, and commitments at a deeper level. As you review the logic model and program plan, take stock of each person or role your program requires. Next, assign an initial category to or primary purpose for each individual's involvement using the following categories.

Building Awareness and Finding Champions

In my experience, implementation managers sometimes fail to gain—and sustain—buy-in from these critical people. When your program is mentioned to someone who should know it or someone you seek to serve as your initiative's champion, you want them to know enough to quickly judge the accuracy of information being presented. You also want them to spread the word about your program and its success when opportunities arise—for example, to potential supporters outside your area or even outside the organization. Ultimately, you want them to support and continue to support your program's ongoing work. But often, it's difficult to gain and hold this group's attention. Worse are cases where their attention is only reached when something goes wrong. That is why the following are critical:

- Identify and acknowledge their important role in your work
- Intentionally define the support you will seek from them and the tactics you will use to ensure that support is and remains present
- Strategize on ways to gain positive attention early on and through early program wins (more on early wins coming up)
- Design targeted messaging that, over time, feeds key information, accomplishments, successes, and impacts

In sum, the implementation manager can define the way support will be obtained and sustained at this preimplementation point. Take the time to plan your strategy and tactics now rather than failing to recognize the inevitable presence and potential influence of these less involved but highly influential program influencers.

Facilitation and Coordination

Another category of people who must support your program is composed of various supporters who, day-to-day, control access to the resources your program requires: operations, custodial staff, HR, and so forth. These are folks who assist in acquiring the necessary "goods" to operate the program, facilitate transportation of participants, make sure those involved get paid, schedule the room or rooms your program requires, house and deliver materials, and generally take care of all the interstices. These are the nonnegotiable things upon which programs rely but which are so often overlooked until something goes wrong.

Initiative Participants

The participants: teachers, students, families, parent coordinators, and so forth.

Often, initiative designers fail to recognize the participants are both participants *and* supporters. They plan and pursue full participation from these folks in the initiative itself but forget to treat them as initiative supporters too.

Now is the time to intentionally plan for their involvement as supporters, just like you've done for our other two categories. Consider what you want them to walk away thinking about the initiative and what you want them to tell others about their experience. Think about how, once engaged, they can positively affect others in support of your program. Oftentimes, initiative participants, as supporters, are helpful in reaching and engaging future participants. They can also be effective advocates in building and sustaining support for the initiative from the leaders in your organization.

Things Going Right

Early on, I asserted that this book was going to be about things gone right and things gone wrong—then right. As you read through this section, you may have sensed me helping you avoid bad things happening. If you did, great. It is true that careful planning can bring that positive result about.

But often, when things go wrong with initiatives, it is because communication is lacking. Sure, there are any number of challenges implementation managers can face on the ground and in the day-to-day operation of the program. But I'm now talking about what's happening "above" the program, with key leaders and the people you need supporting, even bragging about, your work.

It's this situation I'm working to help you avoid. As they say, the best defense is a good offense. I'm suggesting having a deliberate communication plan, educating these individuals about your program—its intent, accomplishments, and impact—and proactively bringing them along.

Armed with awareness and understanding about your program in advance, they will be far more prepared to counter when the inevitable threats to the work arise. So no matter whether it is a budget crisis, a challenge from a funder, a proposed policy change, or simply someone with an axe to grind—whatever the situation, things are far more likely to "go right" when folks are informed enough to advocate for your program.

Early Wins 15

I've had the pleasure of working with many different and diverse programs and clients over the years. Most tend to appreciate my candid and often nontraditional ways of seeing and sharing perspectives.

It is from that perspective that I want to share a couple lessons learned in this section. I think they're helpful ways of reflecting on the work that is perhaps the most important skill any implementation manager can possess. That is, the ability to continuously reflect and improve the work . . . all the while promoting it to everyone involved—within your school, district, and community.

Early Wins

In her book *Leading Change Step-by-Step: Tactics, Tools, and Tales*, Spiro (2012) introduces the idea of **early wins.** She describes phrase as "a term used to describe successes demonstrating concretely that achieving the change goals is feasible and will result in benefits for those involved" (p. 10). Early wins is an especially useful concept for implementation managers. By defining a set of early wins for the program implementation process, you help the team build their individual and collective efficacy while increasing the chances the program will ultimately lead to predictable results.

For example, if the program you are implementing is a new curriculum and our teachers have gone through professional development to prepare for classroom implementation, early wins might be defined as

- Everyone in the school teaching the first lesson
- Success incorporating the curriculum into lesson planning schoolwide
- Students all completing their first assignment and successfully demonstrating their knowledge

By establishing an early win benchmark, reaching it, and then celebrating its achievement, you prove any number of things: The program is relevant, implementation is possible, you are "doing" it with success, and our program can indeed have an impact. What you prove through an early win will vary, so let's look at some different areas in which these wins might be established.

Early Fidelity Wins

Early wins often relate to the stepping stones of program implementation. Far too often, you focus on some larger goal for fidelity at the expense of planning for the many incremental antecedents (i.e., baby steps toward fidelity) that more complex fidelity goals require. For example, if fidelity describes specific implementation targets within a semester or yearly timeframe, our early wins need to define and reward the more discrete steps that lead up to longer goals.

With the help of your logic model or initiative implementation plan, picture the path that leads to full implementation. What are some signposts along the way that could signal you're "on the right track"? Typically, your early wins should be tangible, measurable accomplishments.

Fidelity is often described in terms of amount, time, and quality. Any of these things lends itself to use as an early win. Perhaps the most important element, aside from defining the early win, is promoting that early win goal to everyone involved in the initiative. Early wins will only work if (a) everyone is aware of the target and (b) they "buy into" the effort. I suggest you consider defining early wins for those running the program as well as those who participate. You'll be surprised how an achieved, early win helps get the program's momentum rolling.

Early Equity Wins

You should also consider defining a particular type of early win—equity wins. There are multiple reasons for doing so. Among them is the simple fact that focusing attention on some equity dimension of the program's work typically offers insurance for its attainment. As someone wise once said, "What's measured matters." An early win is naturally something that is measured. It's also carefully watched and monitored. If establishing some dimension of equity is key to your program, then your early wins must accommodate those elements.

What are some of the equity elements that might be the fodder for early wins? Here are some ideas:

- Balanced racial demographics among participants
- Universal access to program and participation—from transportation to any required resources and supports
- Early participation rates reflecting stable participation for all
- Potential early performance metrics that can be broken down by race, grade level, performance level, other status (e.g., English learners)

The idea is this: When you've designed a program that is intended to be equitable across specific, intentional dimensions, you will want to know—early on—that intentional design is coming to fruition. Building early wins around these carefully integrated equity elements helps by focusing attention on critical program dimensions to catch something going right early on. Should that not be the case, you've also provided the earliest opportunity for course correction, which—when successful—can be a win in and of itself. Yes, the snowball analogy applies here as well.

Early Impact Wins

I'll admit that I'm far more likely to be caught advising against early measures of program impact. One of the things my work with programs has proven time and again is this: Key leaders usually have unrealistic expectations about how long it takes to fully implement a program as well as how long it takes to see measurable impact data. So wouldn't "early impact" essentially be an oxymoron?

Successful program leaders carefully *buy* the necessary time to make an impact. This is best accomplished by setting the expectations of those who must support the initiative and providing predefined, early and regular evidence leading up to the targeted set of longer-term outcomes. So often, program designers fail to do so and instead rely on the good nature of key leaders to both understand the time required to achieve impact while also manifesting the patience to wait it out. Unfortunately, in the absence of regular updates and evidence of accomplishments, its far too easy to find a program eliminated before it has had the chance to impact. But early impact wins counter what, in my work, is typically a missed opportunity.

Early impact wins are essentially promising results. Sure, you can measure outputs to show the program's implementation is happening with considerable success. And that is certainly promising. But look to the right-hand side of your logic model and examine the outcomes. How can you apply the concept of early wins to impact?

My strategy involves looking for discrete movement toward the longer-term outcomes. Yes, that might be defined in your short-term outcomes. But often, the length of time required to achieve a short-term outcome defies the patience of the very leaders whose support our initiative requires. You need something definitive to help everyone involved see the earliest impact the program is making. Thus, I challenge you to break down those short-term outcomes into more discrete indicators as a way of intentionally setting up some early impact wins. The accompanying *Tales From the Field* offers a lived example of how this worked quite successfully in a large-scale project I evaluated some time ago.

TALES FROM THE FIELD

Lightspan's Time + Family Involvement + Equity + Motivation (TFEM) = Achievement

In the 1990s, I fell into my first real job as an evaluator. Lightspan was established to offer schools and districts with reading/language arts and mathematics curriculum that could be used in and out of schools with the ultimate goal of increasing student achievement. This was many years before 1:1 laptop or Chromebook programs became prominent and a time where a true technology divide was most notably present in Title I schools.

The formula for success was simple, evidence-based, and elegant. Here's my recreation of Lightspan's theory of action:

If we

- **(T)** Increase the amount of **TIME** spent learning through technology in the home

- **(F)** Increase the involvement of **FAMILIES** in their children's education

- **(E)** Increase **EQUITABLE ACCESS** so that all students have the ability to learn through technology

- **(M)** Increased the **MOTIVATION** of children to not only learn but love to learn

Then

- Students will engage in learning after school
- Families will be more aware and engaged in their children's education
- The digital divide will become a thing of the past
- Children will have a love of learning and choose to engage in their schoolwork

Which will result in

- Increased student achievement in reading/language arts and mathematics

We set out to make the theory of action a reality. Technology-based reading/language arts and mathematics curricula were developed for grades K–6. The programs ran on Sony PlayStations, which were purchased by schools at an incredibly low cost (relative to a mid-1990s laptop) and loaned to students for use at home on the one equitable piece of technology every home had—a television.

As the first programs were implemented in schools across the country, there was more than one school board that questioned the cost and the rather unorthodox approach of a PlayStation-run curriculum. My boss at the time, Bernice Stafford, offered an astute plan to guide our quest for evidence. While establishing the connection between Lightspan's program and high-stakes student achievement measures would take time, every other element of the program could be measured early on. Bernice suggested that we immediately begin by pre- and post-surveying parents and teachers after only a short time, really weeks, of program use.

- Did the TIME dedicated to "learning" at home go up once Lightspan was sent home?
- Did FAMILIES have more interaction with their child's teacher?
- Did the program provide EQUITABLE ACCESS to all students?
- Did parents and teachers judge the students' MOTIVATION for learning to increase as a result of using the program?

(Continued)

(Continued)

These were the key things we investigated early on, after eight weeks of implementation, to offer teachers and schools a data-based early win with their Lightspan program. If these things were indeed happening and the research had already proven that they each contribute significantly to student achievement, then there had to be a positive, student achievement impact "baking" as teachers integrated the curriculum into their practice and students continued to use the program. And, in time, that is exactly what happened.

- By demonstrating early wins, we motivated teachers, parents, and even students to continue their use of the program and, in some cases, double down on the implementation.

- The early wins also bought us time with key leaders—typically, superintendents and school boards—to demonstrate true program efficacy in the form of state test score improvement. The early wins showed we were "on the right track," we should "stay the course," and that, in time, there was good reason to believe that student achievement would result.

- Finally, these early wins differentiated our program from other solutions because of the evidence-based logic on which the program was built and our ability to demonstrate the most discrete of progress measures just eight weeks into program implementation.

As you think about early wins for your program in any of the areas I've described, don't forget their purpose, which is "successes demonstrating concretely that achieving the change goals is feasible and will result in benefits for those involved" (Spiro, 2012, p. 10).

Leadership to Sustain and Promote Programs Over Time

16

Things are up and running. Maybe you're six months into program implementation, or maybe you're six years. Wherever you currently stand in the process of implementing the program, the goal is to remain intentional while engaging in continuous monitoring and improvement. Any program leader will tell you that program implementation is a journey rather than a destination. It would be so convenient if a program could "achieve implementation" and then simply run itself. But much like a plane achieving altitude, keeping things moving forward requires care, attention, and action. One critical aspect of that work is the implementation manager's ongoing advocacy for their program.

Program Advocacy

Wouldn't it be great if the attention you caught and buy-in you established early on, likely through needs assessment data, could naturally be sustained to the point of program implementation? Unfortunately, it's inevitable that other needs and programs will catch the eye of your organization. There will be temptations to move on to new and novel needs and requests.

To sustain their interest and support, you'll need to carefully plan for some ongoing promotion of your program. That will naturally involve its implementation progress, accomplishments, and early return on investment. The goal is to send attention-getting bits of information to program supporters on a regular basis. As the program leader and the person who knows most about each aspect of the program, you are the right person to control the conversation.

Rather than waiting for someone to ask a question or request information, you must serve as your program's public relations agent. Here are some ideas to consider:

- Offer regular updates in bulleted form to describe program accomplishments and milestones.

- Tie your ongoing dissemination to things you know these important and potential supporters are grappling with—in other words, if your program is helping meet a strategic goal or addressing part of an emotionally charged contemporary issue, concisely summarize that contribution within the larger context.

- Produce an infographic that depicts your outputs and outcomes—and your accomplishments in each. A one-glance reporting of key results may receive more attention from high-level leaders when compared to narrative descriptions.

- Consider all the ways your program is producing a return on the organization's investment—including positive returns that you didn't anticipate early on but which have been realized as a result of the program's implementation.

- Formulate your program's public relations campaign with next steps in mind. If you're contemplating program expansion or add-on or scaling the program into other settings, position your ongoing campaign to support where you plan to head—both short and long term.

As I've said, you have the chance to control the narrative about your program when you take deliberate steps to do so. However, implementation managers so often fail to control the narrative. They keep their heads down, feeling the success that comes from dutifully implementing the program and seeing its impact on participants. There is nothing wrong with this. In fact, it is the typical emphasis of a successful program leader.

But all the while their heads are down, things are changing above, to the point they receive a request to justify their program's resources or even notice that a decision has been made to eliminate the program. Many a program has been shut down because of necessary supporters/leaders lacking information and being left to develop their own opinions about the program, its implementation, and its impact.

Avoiding the Point of Crisis

I've been called into projects at the very point where a successful program is on the chopping block. Inevitably what I find is that those whose support is needed, namely key leaders, haven't had their expectations set early on, nor have they received information to inform their thinking about all aspects of the program. So how can you help in these crisis situations?

- Start by taking an inventory of anything and everything the program has documented. That includes the needs assessment data, the program plan and logic model, research or other elements of the knowledge base on which the program has been based, output data, and any evidence of outcomes that has been collected.

- Next, work with the team to identify things you *could know* in the short term and the value of each. For example, if process/output data could be obtained, how would it be received? Would leadership be impressed by the numbers of people involved, or would it just lead to the inevitable question about impact? We make strategic decisions about where to invest our limited time to document the program and its worth.

- In many ways, this is a time when you become the program's public relations agent as you seek to understand it, uncover any and all evidence of its value, and then put together a campaign that presents your findings.

Take careful note: Evidence isn't limited to results. The deliberate design of your program and its attentiveness to the true need of an important population that should matter to these leaders is also a key information component that you must share. Good design, predicated on established needs, yields to predictable results. You want to showcase this fact to the decision-makers and then demonstrate how your program is doing exactly that: working toward, then achieving, predicable results.

This sort of retrospective public relations campaign—including priority evaluation results—has spared many a program. I've come to believe it really is a matter of helping people understand the value of a good program but doing so in a way that matches how they look at the organization and world. I've also concluded that the point of crisis often wouldn't have been reached if the program leader had been attending to the necessary public relations ongoing programs require.

So here's to the program leaders who are, rightly, looking down as they care for, understand, and improve their programs. But here's to the program leaders who are also looking up, advocating for their programs, and controlling the narrative around their work. That's part of expertly navigating the white space in the organization to the full benefit of your program and its participants.

Advice for Scaling Programs 17

While it might be premature at this point to consider scaling the emerging program you've just crafted, I still want to offer some insight on the topic. This is because many of the ideas around scaling programs I find to be just as relevant to implementing programs. Now is also a good time to consider the following facts about scaling programs, if you have even the slightest expectation that the program you're creating will eventually be scaled. By doing so, you'll position yourself when you reach the time for scaling.

When I use the term **scaling**, I'm describing the effort that takes a program from its initial implementation and setting and expands it to additional implementations—even new and novel ones. That might mean taking a one-classroom program and replicating it across the school. It could also mean taking a one-school program and expanding it to a cluster of schools or the entire district. It also applies to taking a districtwide program and scaling it to districts across the country. In essence, scaling is about expanding the program's use. That often means expansion into new and contextually different settings.

Fidelity and Flexibility

I will admit that, when I think about fidelity, I first think of true and unwavering commitment to some set of requirements. Yes, I fear I'm a rule follower. That trait, for me, appears to come with a, perhaps overly, cautious level of allegiance to defined expectations. Put me on a diet, and I'm going to count every last calorie in my food and every last minute of exercise I complete. In my mind, I cannot imagine anything worse than making the commitment yet not exactly following the dictated process to the point where the defined impact isn't realized. Once again, it all goes back to predictable results.

I think this is one reason why I enjoy evaluating programs. In doing so, I get to see the relationships between action and impact so vividly. For that reason, it came as a rather big surprise to find both fidelity and flexibility regularly mentioned under the topic of program scalability.

Yet flexibility is requisite when scaling a program for many reasons. Perhaps the most logical is the simple fact that the context into which the scaled program will be placed may differ, greatly, from the context in which it was initially created. For me, I'm used to moving from needs to programs, which is what I've shared in this book. But there are times when established programs come to us and we must implement them as successfully as possible but within the context we're given.

I've come to think about the scaling of programs like training to run a race. Just like programs should have defined fidelity measures, so too does the defined training regimen that leads up to running a half-marathon, let's say. An established program comes with defined, proven elements that guide its implementation that were born of its original context. When a program moves to scale and meets with a new context, it's like reaching race day and running the race. Sure, your training will pay off . . . but you will also find yourself observing and adapting to the environment and circumstances around you to optimize your performance. Similarly, scaling a program involves being flexible with fidelity measures, but it doesn't mean throwing them out the window. Rather, an expert implementation manager is challenged to balance fidelitous implementation with necessary flexibility such that the program can successfully operate within its new context.

When considering scaling a program, it's important to be mindful of the program's original design because it influences how the program is scaled. Consider these two scenarios:

- Programs that are homegrown and designed by those who will implement it should consider scalability and, in essence, be "baking in" flexibility for scalability, assuming that is a likely future need.

- Programs being adopted are the more traditional situation, where an existing program is purchased and intended for school- or district-wide implementation. Here too, studies suggest the need to refine programs for context, again requiring flexibility, otherwise, they'll become "caricatures" of their original design as they increasingly become a square peg being jammed into a round hole (Elmore, 1996).

Program Leader as Change Agent

I've previously discussed the fact that program leaders are change agents. Implementing a program, without a doubt, requires change. How well people adapt to that change will, in part dictate the program's success.

Effectively supporting change is critical to scaling or expanding any program. It is something that must be fully planned and carefully executed as part of any program expansion. Writing about curriculum reforms of the mid-twentieth century, Elmore (1996) observes that program developers had assumed that "good" curriculum and teaching practice were self-explanatory and self-implementing. Once teachers and school administrators recognized the clearly superior ideas embodied in the new curricula, they would simply switch from traditional textbooks to the new materials and change long-standing practices to improve their teaching and the chances of their students succeeding in school.

So that didn't happen. Elmore's insight to change is remarkable because the scenario he describes is something I've encountered many times when evaluating "good" programs across school districts. For me, this type of scenario goes back to the human performance model and the simple fact that, if people don't see value in making a change while also being confident they can be successful in doing so, then it is unlikely that change will occur—and, even if change begins, predictable results are far from guaranteed.

These perspectives point to the clear need to intentionally plan for change. Additionally, they demonstrate how unrealistic it is to expect things to naturally change on their own volition. Scaling a program and bringing it to a group of people and context requires similar amounts of planning and care when compared to the new program development process we have discussed.

Common Challenges to Scaling Up Programs

The challenges of implementation with a scaled-up program tend to mirror those of first-run programs. But let's take a moment to review them here. These challenges include the following:

- Lack of buy-in and failure to set clear expectations from key leaders and necessary supporters

- Implementation managers who lack readiness to facilitate change—including the necessary skills and knowledge, available time, and/or motivation to accomplish the work

- Failure to recognize the true amount of time needed to accomplish program implementation to the point of impact, and no attention to early wins that sustain the interest of key leaders and initiative supporters, motivate the continued implementation for participants, and offer opportunities for early course correction when necessary

DID YOU KNOW? SCALING SMARTLY

When programs are scaled to sites (schools, classrooms) where they fail, that lack of success is often the result of things completely unrelated to the program itself. Often, these sites came with an existing context that was simply inhospitable to the program's introduction (Marshall, 2005).

Whether infrastructure or culture, people attempting to scale programs are well advised to conduct a needs assessment, specific to the program's implementation within the new context to anticipate how factors in place will both accelerate and deter the program's presence. It's easy to assume that a program that is working in one site will naturally work in a similar site. However, such assumptions fail to systemically consider the true range of factors.

I especially like the way Clarke et al. (2006) differentiate between the *intervention* (e.g., program) and the *conditions for success* when exploring scalability. They liken these dimensions of scalability to antibiotics:

> For instance, the effective use of antibiotics illustrates the concept of "conditions for success": Antibiotics are a powerful "design," but worshiping the vial that holds them or rubbing the ground-up pills all over one's body or taking all the pills at once are ineffective strategies for usage—only administering pills at specified intervals works as an implementation strategy. (p. 32)

If nothing else, my hope is that you've seen how careful needs assessment, followed by deliberate planning, leads to predictable results. If so, your takeaway from this timeout is simply this: The same goes for scaling a program.

Wrap-Up for Part II

Lessons in Leadership, Inventing the Initiative

Linda was feeling great about her needs assessment results. More importantly—Linda's team was feeling engaged in the initiative. Successful needs assessment has a way of doing that as you connect with the people involved and your desire to make things better—along with your connection to the work—grows.

Leadership Matters

The sections you've just read explored program design and program leadership. On the topic of leadership and being a champion for your initiative, let's take a moment to observe what Linda has been doing with this work from the moment you met her. She has been involving people, including engaging a significant-sized team who then engaged sites, leaders, educators, families, and community partners.

Something else she's been doing is regularly talking up the work to the people sitting on the floor above her. The fact she found that parents of English learners are far less likely to engage she shared that up (to the superintendent and cabinet), and she shared that across—to her colleagues in English Learner Services, Community Engagement, and Curriculum. But she isn't the only one talking things up. Remember that team of fifteen? Each one of them is out there, day-to-day, talking up the project and little-by-little paving the way for change.

Oh—if you're wondering whether all this is planned, well the answer is of course! When I chat with Linda, she calls it "Program PR," like it is no big deal. But she fully knows what she is doing and how it goes far beyond public relations. When I watch her operate and think about it at the macro-level, Linda is basically running the initiative before it is even defined! What's more—people respond! They get on board, they catch the excitement, they share responsibility for the gaps, and they co-sign onto the solution. Magic? Nope. Leadership.

What's the Plan

In addition to all the "white space" work Linda is busy doing—which is the job of any initiative leader—you can learn from what Linda and her team did, in terms of their initiative design process. Here's how things unfolded:

- The team took their needs assessment results—including the handful of the "headlines"—and socialized them around the district. By "socialized," I mean that each of the fifteen team members shared the results with people around them. They invited people to respond to the results and considered that feedback as they moved into the initiative design phase.

- Next, they defined the initiative's elements. Initially, they found it helpful to brainstorm a handful of program elements they knew would be needed. Those initial buckets were the following:

  o Family Involvement Program Curriculum

  o Family Involvement Educator Development

  o Classroom and School Implementation Support

  o Family Engagement Toolkit Integration

  o Community Connections

- They then used the Logic Model tool (Tool 7) to define the inputs, processes and outputs, and outcomes that would, together, become the initiative. Look at what the team came up with on the pages that follow.

Observations

I trust you are, like I am, impressed when you see that logic model. You're able to note the detail that exists while keeping the description at a high enough level to consume. You can imagine this logic model being used in team meetings to guide planning. And I can assure you that it served as the input for producing the team's detailed initiative plan.

A Step Closer to Fidelity Definition

Another thing I'd like to highlight about this logic model is how it pushed the team toward defining fidelity for the initiative. Fidelity defines the "right" way to implement the initiative. Figure 17.1 and Table 17.1 together provide a brief overview that connects the team's ideas about the various elements of fidelity as presented in their logic model.

Figure 17.1 Logic Model for Linda and Team's Family Engagement Initiative

Family Engagement Program: Initial Logic Model

INPUTS

- Recent curriculum reform and leadership capacity-building that incorporates family engagement components

- Comprehensive needs assessment results to guide family engagement initiative focus

- Leadership commitment to initiative resources—personnel and budget

- Continuous monitoring and improvement via data targeted to outputs and outcomes

PROCESS

Targeted Initiative Intensity

- Across all initiative elements, intensify focus on currently underserved families of English learner and BIPOC students

- Leverage survey and interview results to focus engagement on issues that matter most to parents

Build Capacity District-Wide

- Build educator knowledge of, value and confidence for, family engagement

- Train educators and site leadership to activate family engagement elements in existing curriculum

- Each educator and site leader establishes personal action plan for implementing family engagement in upcoming school year

Connect and Engage Families

- Implement action plans across school year

OUTPUTS

- Training, actions plans, and supports all intentionally include differentiated supports for parents of English learners and BIPOC children

- Engagement focus, including monthly theme, matches needs assessment data and findings

- All school staff and leaders trained by qualified staff prior to start of academic year

- Each classroom educator and site leader has completed and reviewed action plan for family engagement—including curriculum and community partner connections

- Site leaders confirm action plans are carried out

OUTCOMES

Initial (Month 1)

- Lessons leverage existing family engagement components in curriculum (Teachers, Site Leaders)

- At least 50% of families respond to invitations for interaction (Teachers, Site Leaders)

Short Term (Month 2 though mid-year)

- Lessons continue to leverage family engagement components in curriculum

- Action plans are fully implemented and successful teaching practice modifications are documented

- At least 60% of families, on average, are having a defined interaction with school personnel on a monthly basis

Midterm (End of Year 1)

- Relevant metrics described above

- At least 60% of families, on average, are having a defined interaction with school personnel on a monthly basis

- Defined interactions demonstrate reduced variance based on race and socio-economic status

(Continued)

(Continued)

INPUTS

PROCESS

- Site leader feedback
- Establish a monthly engagement theme, prompting at least one connection between every family and school every month

Engage Community Organizations as Partners and to Extend Messaging (faith-based, social services, park and recreation, etc.)

- Recruit and sustain community partners for engagement
- Coordinate messaging using monthly engagement theme
- Unified messaging provides for maximum impact and reach within multiple organizations and agencies

OUTPUTS

- Action plans are regularly reviewed by site staff for quality, progress, adjustment, and accountability
- Engagement themes are integrated into action plan
- At least 15 key partners are recruited and in place prior to school year
- Partners receive and disseminate coordinated messaging by the 7th day of each month
- Families connect with school, prompted by community partners

OUTCOMES

- Parent surveys reflect at least a 10% increase in confidence and value for engaging with school
- Community partners can describe at least three benefits observed that result from the first year's engagement effort participation

Long Term (End of Year 2)

- Relevant metrics described above
- At least 85% of families, on average, are having a defined interaction with school personnel on a monthly basis
- Defined interactions demonstrate reduce do not vary significantly based on race nor socio-economic status
- 80% of parent surveys indicate a high level of confidence and value for engaging with school
- Parent survey responses do not vary significantly based on race nor socio-economic status
- School-by-school engagement among community partners and families deepens beyond the family engagement effort

Table 17.1 Fidelity Table	
FIDELITY ELEMENT	**FINDING IT IN THE TEAM'S LOGIC MODEL**
Expectations—specific to the content, frequency, duration, and coverage of the initiative's implementation	Look to the Outputs column, which defines expectations in measurable terms. For example • Engagement focus, including monthly theme, matches needs assessment data and findings • All school staff and leaders trained prior to start of academic year • Each classroom educator and site leader has completed and reviewed action plan for family engagement—including curriculum and community partner connections
Dose—of initiative in which participants are required to engage to benefit (establish dosage boundaries to define successful participation)	Look to the Outcomes column for dosage expectations. For example: • Parents having defined interactions with school personnel on a monthly basis. • Daily lessons leverage family engagement components. Additionally, action plans would allow teachers to customize their approach, including dosage—but it needs to be specific and measurable.
Quality—of initiative implementation (e.g., quality of leadership, program oversight, coaching, teaching, etc.)	Look to the Outputs column, which defines success in terms of implementation quality. For example: • Quality of training measured through assigned personnel and impact • Quality review of action plans by site leaders
Reactions of People Involved—how we intend to ensure our teachers and students—or whomever the initiative engages—find relevance in their participation	Look to Process column. For example • Leverage survey and interview results to focus engagement on issues that matter most to parents • Each educator and site leader establishes personal action plan for implementing family engagement in upcoming school year
Initiative Differentiation—how we intend to make certain our initiative is unique and different from others that may address similar outcomes	Look to Process and Outcomes columns. For example • Across all initiative elements, intensify focus on currently underserved families of English learner and BIPOC students • School-by-school engagement among community partners and families deepens beyond the family engagement effort

The logic model cannot attend to each of these areas in depth without going beyond the high-level initiative picture it is intended to provide. The initiative plan, therefore, becomes the place to further elaborate these fidelity elements.

But My Initiative Doesn't Go Beyond the Classroom Walls

I've chosen to highlight Linda's rather large and arguably high-level initiative, to give you a living example of how the process can be followed. Of course, the various initiative design activities can be readily scaled down. I've seen teachers use this process to develop classroom initiatives of all sorts—from integrated learning across STEAM elements to classroom recycling programs that involve content across the curriculum. Site leaders have done similar scaling down at their schools. So it is important to note that the process is perfectly scalable, and the elements can be far fewer, yet the guidance still applies. In fact, that's especially true for early wins.

The Team's Early Wins

Before we leave Linda and the team, I want to note the team's careful attention to early wins. I fear, in some ways, I may have painted a rather rosy picture of the team's work. So let's acknowledge that sometimes people don't respond as you'd like. Sometimes, people won't participate in the data collection. And sometimes, you just want to give up. Again, Linda's leadership acknowledges the challenges, sees them for what they are, and still champions the team forward, which results in far more good days than bad. There are specific things you can "program" into initiatives that help stay the course once the initiative is in full swing. That's exactly what the team did.

You'll note that Linda's logic model doesn't begin with Year 1 outcomes. Rather, it starts with outcomes that can be marked and celebrated after the very first month! The team went on to develop outcomes at discrete intervals (Month 2 through midyear, Year 1, Year 2). The team set early outcomes that could be attained without too much effort and then celebrated the heck out of them. This gets the momentum going—even for those who didn't meet the Month 1 outcomes, as they see their peers succeeding and celebrating.

PART II: DISCUSSION QUESTIONS

Use these questions to check your understanding or share your learnings with your initiative team.

1. What components do successful logic models include?

2. How can leaders use a logic model to successfully lead initiative design?

3. What are the typical components that comprise "fidelity?"

4. What are some of the strategies that leaders can use to successfully "attach" an initiative to their existing organization?

5. Why are early wins a necessary component of successful initiatives?

6. When scaling an initiative in a new or novel setting, how do leaders ensure consistency of impact?

PACING YOUR DESIGN EFFORT

Initiative design and implementation is the largest phase of this work. How long should it take to design an initiative? Similar to my suggestions for needs assessment, the necessary time investment is flexible, to a degree.

Short answer: With successful needs assessment data in hand, your design effort should take less time. That's because your keen focus on needs and strengths immediately limits the range of things you can and should do.

Long answer: A full understanding of the current situation, coupled with a detailed statement of the ideal, sets you up to design a responsive program. Knowing both strengths and barriers further focuses what your design will include. My advice is to make a solid investment in initiative design,

(Continued)

(Continued)

such that a thoughtful, implementation-informed initiative results. However, with your commitment to follow-through on monitoring and continuous improvement, you will have opportunities to hone the design over time.

Table 17.2 provides some advice about initiative design investments based upon the time you have available.

Table 17.2 Pacing Your Initiative Design	
IF YOU'RE ABLE TO INVEST . . .	**HERE'S WHAT I RECOMMEND YOU DO FOR INITIATIVE DESIGN**
A Few Days	1. Refresh your understanding with a walk through the needs assessment results 2. Bring together a thought partner or two to brainstorm ideas 3. Consider each barrier that has been identified and use the Solutions Based on Barriers and Strengths tool to consider a range of responsive initiative elements 4. Use the Logic Model Building tool as a brainstorm collector, as you identify resources you will need, the different elements or activities your initiative will include, and the outcomes you will use to judge success 5. Work iteratively to refine the plan as you reflect and then make adjustments based on your evolving understanding and thought partners' input 6. Intentionally place "early wins" in the initiative design 7. Document the initial plan in a logic model and then supplement the logic model with additional detail, if necessary, using the categories of information in the Initiative Plan Schematic tool
A Few Weeks	Use the few-day ideas, but also 1. Sustain your needs assessment team and leverage their support for initiative design 2. Expand the brainstorming and reflection opportunities to unfold over multiple sessions, with time for thinking and reflection between design meetings

IF YOU'RE ABLE TO INVEST . . .	HERE'S WHAT I RECOMMEND YOU DO FOR INITIATIVE DESIGN
	3. Engage in some "show and tell" opportunities by sharing a current initiative design with those outside your team for feedback and bring insight back to the team to inform the iterative design process
	4. When you reach a final, proposed design, dedicate time to compare the design back to all of your needs assessment data and ask yourself, "Will this address each of our needs while also leveraging the strengths we found?"
	5. Follow guidance in the Initiative Plan Schematic to document your initiative effort at an appropriate level, based on those who you anticipate needing information
A Month or More	Use the few-days and few-week ideas, but also
	1. Expand the timeframe during which your initiative is designed
	2. Expand the range of thought partners with whom you consult on the design
	3. Consider hosting a series of design workshops with a variety of people who will have insight, from potential initiative participants to those who will oversee or manage the implementation
	4. Move from broad ideas about the initiative's design toward consensus across your thought partners
	5. Socialize the initial logic model and initiative plan with potential participants, implementers, and those whose support you will need (Champions)
	6. Draft and develop guidance using the Initiative Plan Schematic by documenting at a level of detail necessary to both gain support from leadership for the initiative and also guide implementation efforts

From Implementation to Impact

Implementing an initiative without any sort of evaluation is like sending your 18-year-old off into the world and never hearing from them again. Did your investments help them succeed in the world? Program evaluation allows us to not only see our initiatives in action but to also document their impacts—from the planned and expected to the amazing and unexpected.

ASSESS
STRENGTHS
& NEEDS

EVALUATE
INITIATIVE

Predictable Results

Strengths & Needs

DATA

DESIGN
INITIATIVE

IMPLEMENT
INITIATIVE

In Part III You Will . . .

- Explore monitoring and improving your initiative over time
- Create an evaluation plan to investigate your initiative's implementation and impact
- Define evaluation questions to guide inquiry
- Assess what you can and should evaluate now and into the future
- Organize findings in ways that "speak" to your colleagues and thought partners
- Use evaluation findings to demonstrate impact and underscore your initiative advocacy

 Key Tools

Tool 11: Evaluation Plan Sections

Tool 12: Evaluation Question Criteria

Tool 13: Presenting Evaluation Questions

Tool 14: Data Collection Methods for Program Evaluation

Tool 15: Matching Evaluation Questions to Data Sources

Tool 16: Summarizing Data Collection Methods

Tool 17: Evaluation Question and Learnings Inventory

Tool 18: Organizing Evaluation Findings

Tool 19: Making Results Useful

Self-Assessment: Implementation and Impact

Use this quick self-assessment to help you determine your prior knowledge for topics covered in Part III: From Implementation to Impact.

HOW MUCH DO YOU KNOW ABOUT . . .	A LOT	A LITTLE	NOT AT ALL	UNSURE
• Continuous monitoring and adjustment	O	O	O	O
• Benefits of program evaluation for leaders	O	O	O	O
• Course correction for initiatives	O	O	O	O
• Writing complete evaluation questions	O	O	O	O
• Presenting evaluation results	O	O	O	O
• The relationship between needs assessment and program evaluation	O	O	O	O

Continuous Monitoring and Adjustment 18

In this final part of this book, the emphasis is increasingly focused on understanding the initiative's operation and impact. It's probably been twenty-five years since I heard the term **continuous monitoring and adjustment**. Since that time, I've probably used it in every grant program proposal I've authored. You see, no amount of needs assessment nor careful program design can account for every nuance, barrier, or reality that will be met when "program meets world." The efforts I've described in this book are all designed to increase the chance of predictable results. But our vigilance pursuing predictable results doesn't end on program launch.

Continuous monitoring and adjustment recognizes what successful initiative leaders naturally do. They see their program's implementation as a journey. They ask good questions of participants and others involved in the initiative over the natural course of their work. They're continuously assessing how the program is operating through both informal inquiry and more formal program evaluation efforts. They build out their understanding of the initiative from all angles, which informs the smaller and larger adjustments they make over time.

How do you accomplish this work? Our journey through initiatives is now turning to program evaluation. Program evaluation offers the chance to understand the program's operation and to document its impact. But aside from the more formalized evaluation efforts, let's also recognize that within the daily operation of any program, you have many opportunities to "check the pulse" of the program, ask questions, hear perspectives, offer "what if" scenarios to thought partners, and to benefit from their perspectives. I like to think of this endeavor as collecting in-formative data because these data are both "informal" and "formative." The thought of doing it may seem complex, but it begins with simply adopting a commitment to inquiry and then following through as you ask questions, make observations, and continuously assess the initiative in the real world.

Formative data offers insight into the program experience, from its implementation to its reception and application by participants. Your knowledge of defined implementation fidelity, coupled with an understanding of both short- and long-term outcomes, places you—the implementation manager—in a unique place to conduct this inquiry. You are also the person who has the authority to make mid-course adjustments to the program when you see they are needed.

Continuous Monitoring and Improvement

Efforts to continuously monitor and improve the program are the natural next step in any program's operation and oversight. Here, you use the evaluation plan as well as your day-to-day observations in running the program to identify strengths of the program both in its successful implementation and across the outcomes you're pursuing—even the earliest indications of progress toward outcomes. What if something isn't going right? Apply your needs assessment expertise to figure out why. Here too, our barriers and strengths categories from Part I can inform what you do.

Program Care and Nurturing

In most cases, when you identify a strength you want to document it and build upon it. When you uncover a barrier, you will want to understand its cause or causes and work to eliminate whatever is holding you back from realizing complete implementation and your carefully defined outcomes.

It is normal for course correction to be required. Sometimes, repeated corrections are necessary to iteratively "fit" the program to the participants and organization. After all, people and organizations are dynamic; to think adjustment won't be required means convincing yourself both people and organizations do not change. Initiative leaders anticipate the need for adjustment by keeping their eyes open, reviewing all evaluation data available, and posing questions to the people implementing the program as well as the program participants. That free flow of information and opinion serves them well as they anticipate challenges and address them before they rise to a true level of concern.

Let's take a closer look at program course changes.

Connecting the Dots

One typical adjustment program leaders encounter involves the making of connections. Often, on paper and in concept, the initiative elements fit nicely together. They all make logical sense—you even have proven it in your logic model!

Yet, when program meets world, those elements may not come together as naturally as you envisioned. Or it may simply be that the people implementing the program lack the bigger, integrated picture and need to be brought along in order to execute their roles in a coordinated fashion.

I call this "connecting the dots" because the adjustment may be as simple as deliberately sharing the larger program plan and the logic of its operation with the team. Now you may say, "I already did that early on, as part of program planning." If you did, that was exactly the right thing to do. But take a moment to appreciate how those early ideas can be completely lost as program meets world and any number of context-based factors come into play.

Working with the program day-to-day offers an incredibly new and rich context. It is one where focus is mostly given to immediate and pressing needs rather than the "bigger picture" of what the program set out to accomplish. It may be time to pull the team together, celebrate the lived experience they've gained through the program's early operation (think, early win), and, together, do some dot connecting to remind them of the larger program plan, logic, and quest for outcomes.

As you make this investment, why not also spend some time elaborating how elements of the team's work contributes to the larger outcomes? Reviewing the connections between team member roles while highlighting where one role relies upon and benefits from another is also a good idea. This type of review and opportunity to connect or reconnect is often critical at this point, once everyone has "lived" the program and its implementation for some amount of time.

TALES FROM THE FIELD: CORRECTING THE DOTS

This term was coined, at least for me, by Dr. Peggy O'Brien. She is, perhaps, my favorite initiative collaborator over the better part of two decades. She has engaged me in work, from nationwide public broadcasting education initiatives to her current role directing the Folger Shakespeare Library's education programs.

One day, while knee-deep in a program that was one-part complex and one-part vexing, we were reviewing where we'd been and comparing that to what we were attempting to do. If you just identified that as "connecting the dots," you're absolutely correct. That's what we thought we were sitting down to do. Although, at the time, we didn't formally name the task as such.

After probably forty-five minutes of discussion and the sharing of in-formative data from partners and participants in this program, we both leaned back, and maybe, I rolled my eyes. Peggy thought silently to herself, and to break that silence, I asked, "What are you thinking?" She replied, "I'm just trying to correct the dots." Well, following a shared, robust round of laughter, it struck me: Yes! That's exactly what we were doing. Freudian slip or not, we were faced with correcting the dots because we simply couldn't connect them as we had originally planned.

One significant dot we corrected was the role of a community partner. While the organizations involved shared a rich history and, on paper, similar missions, it was downright apparent mid-initiative that the partnership wasn't producing the anticipated results. In fact, we realized the partnership didn't have the capacity to achieve the envisioned results. We pursued dot correction in terms of who was the "right" partner and what the "right" role and contributions needed to be.

Sometimes course correction is what's required. While "correcting the dots" may require more time and thinking, it is important to recognize when it is the right—maybe only—thing to do. You'll know this to be the case based on any number of signs, which could include the following:

- Implementing the program with planned fidelity becomes impossible.

- Your supporters lose interest in the program as designed, and you cannot regain support.

- Needs change in significant ways, and your defined outcomes no longer align.

- Your program, unplanned of course, steps onto the "turf" of another program doing the same or similar work, and the duplication of effort must be addressed.

- Resources originally planned to be available are no longer present.

When this happens, it's time to revisit your logic model and explore revisions to the program's design, operation, and outcomes. In my experience, this process isn't really that different from earlier stages of program design. You return to an abbreviated needs assessment phase, benefitting from both the original and any new contextual data you might quickly collect, and work again toward optimal program design. If you've been monitoring the program, asking questions, trying on "what if" scenarios surrounding the program's operation, then you are probably already close to knowing, in a data-informed way, what corrective action is needed.

Expanding the Dots

Here's a final "adjustment" that you or whomever is leading your initiative would feel lucky to face. It typically comes with demonstrated success. One day, you receive an email, telephone call, or announcement from a funder that they have extra money they'd like to award you to expand your program. Yes, it is a good problem to face . . . and it does happen!

"Expanding the dots" typically requires a little connecting and a little correcting (or perhaps reimagining) of the dots. It involves connecting the dots because initiative expansion usually builds upon what you're already doing with success by connecting to what's already happening. It corrects the dots by requiring expanded outcomes through its support to address additional needs that were previously out-of-scope. Connecting to the existing initiative benefits the team through a "jump start" toward implementation rather than requiring a return to the starting point.

When faced with such an opportunity, my advice is always to revisit your needs assessment data, take stock of what your current program is accomplishing versus the remaining needs, and work to identify the next highest priority. Your choices here are typically

- Going deeper—by enhancing what is already present
- Going wider—by attaching something completely new yet logically related to the current program

Your needs assessment data, coupled with early results from the existing program, should light the way to what's right for your participants and organization.

Program Evaluation Planning 19

What an adventure we've had! Your careful planning has led to a true understanding of your participants. You've listened to and integrated their voice, vision, and viewpoints into the initiative you've created. Implementation has begun. You're collecting "in-formative" data to learn, informally, from people's experiences with the program—be they your program implementation team members or participants. That in-formative data is supporting your early efforts to monitor and continuously improve the program's operation.

I started this book with the intent to help you achieve programs that yield predictable results. As you now know, all the work that led up to this point was done with deference to that intended outcome: ensuring predictable results. So now our efforts turn to confirming those results are indeed present.

This part of the book provides guidance about evaluation knowing and doing. From this point forward, you are going to operate in full evaluation mode. "But I'm not an Evaluator!"

I can imagine some folks at this point saying, "But I'm not an evaluator!" Or "This sounds complicated." I'll agree to a point: Program evaluation isn't a pursuit to take lightly. But I'm equally of the opinion that anyone can choose to care about their program's operation and impact. Anyone can choose to plan for and collect data in support of running the best program possible and, just as important, demonstrating its success. This is what effective leaders naturally do and should continue doing—especially with initiatives. Leaders have an obligation to make the programs in schools the best they can be. Program evaluation offers the means by which that obligation is fulfilled.

You may not have the luxury of access to an external or professional evaluator. But that's no reason to skip an investment in program evaluation. You've come all this way; it would be a shame not to confirm the predictable results your program was designed to achieve.

Getting Started With Program Evaluation

I've conducted program evaluations on over $130 million dollars worth of funded programs within the United States and internationally. I've also been involved in the needs assessment, design, and implementation of countless more, in various roles—from program designer to implementation lead. Those adventures have led me to a handful of evaluation "truisms" I've learned through practice (Table 19.1). Many of these things aren't what you'd learn from the typical book on program evaluation. Rather, they're the kind of "street smarts" that come from doing evaluation in the real world. Whether evaluating a program, product, or policy, these learnings resonate each time I'm working with leaders who want to better understand their initiatives and impact through evaluation investments. I hope you will find them motivating. I also encourage you to find them helpful in reducing any concerns you might face at the thought of pursuing evaluation with your team.

Table 19.1   7 Program Evaluation Truisms

1	**If nothing else—waste no time and do no harm:** Collect only the data you fully intend to use; focus your questions on key outcomes; and be ever-considerate of your respondent's time. Use unobtrusive measures whenever possible. For example, make use of existing data or leverage participant-completed materials used in a program as data collection opportunities.
2	**Use outcomes for your evaluation work:** Use predetermined outcomes when you can; if none exist, deconstruct the program/product to define outcomes. Gain consensus about the stated outcomes from each stakeholder before initiating an evaluation effort.
3	**Determine the coin of the realm and measure it:** Dedicate the necessary time to determine the most persuasive, valuable evidence for your stakeholder(s), and prioritize your evaluation efforts accordingly. Design your evaluation so that, regardless of your findings, each stakeholder receives some benefit.
4	**Know that apples may have to be compared to oranges**: When all else fails, accept this simple fact. Your work may call for comparing measurably different programs or data from less than perfect samples. Admit it, understand it, state it . . . and proceed.
5	**It's never too early to plan or measure—embed evaluation from the start:** Use evaluation to prove needs and/or establish the current state (baseline data). Evaluate pilot or prototype versions of your program (formative evaluation). Consider evaluation as a natural part of program design and implementation rather than something you do once the program is fully implemented.
6	**Prepare for imperfection . . . it is inevitable:** A survey question may be misworded or misinterpreted by respondents, or you may not be able to attract the sample size you desire. The whole program might change mid-evaluation! Do your best but know that no evaluation is perfect. Realizing what you could have done differently or alternate questions you could have asked is a typical outcome of any evaluation effort.
7	**Learn by doing:** If you're a novice at evaluation, give it a try. Practice helps you learn and develop your evaluation prowess. Experienced evaluators perfect their skills with every program they evaluate—and so can you.

The Evaluation Plan 20

As you contemplate how you will evaluate your program, I'll share some good news with you: The logic model you've invested time and energy to create will pay off in dividends at this point.

As a program evaluator, it would be far easier for me to count the times I've been asked to evaluate a program with no logic model, relative to the very, very few times I've come onto the scene and been handed one to support my work. We talked about it being both a road map and a place mat. It defines the outcomes the program has been designed to achieve while also telling us the exact processes that will be used to get there.

So again I will say, let's hear it for the logic model. It's going to provide an ideal "input" as you move forward to develop an evaluation plan.

Elements of a Successful Evaluation Plan

Much like the logic model and related program plan direct your program, the **evaluation plan** will direct your evaluation inquiry. Separate from the program plan, it is intended to guide your efforts to document the program's actual implementation and impact. The evaluation plan is responsive to the program plan but separate because it provides an objective investigation of the program's operation and impact.

Let's begin by outlining some of the typical elements you can expect to find in an evaluation plan. This will provide the foundation for building your plan as you explore some of the more detailed evaluation plan elements in the following sections. Those elements include everything from evaluation models to frame your inquiry to guidance for evaluation questions and instrument design.

Evaluation Plan Sections

The first evaluation planning tool (Tool 11) describes the elements you'll find in most evaluation plans. Think of it as a "to-do" list for building your plan. You likely have much of the background information already sitting in your logic model and program plan. Feel free to repurpose it for the relevant evaluation plan sections.

TOOL 11: EVALUATION PLAN SECTIONS	
Purpose	Define relevant sections of a successful evaluation plan.
Task	Use this tool to anticipate the information you will cover in your evaluation plan and to begin conceptualizing your evaluation plan document. Moderate the level of detail based on the size of your initiative (school-based versus districtwide and beyond). Think about who might read the plan and write with the most unfamiliar reader in mind.
SECTION	**DESCRIPTION AND GUIDANCE**
Introduction	A short and concise overview of the program and need for evaluation. This section should also name the organization.
Program Description	Provides descriptions of the following: Organization: a bit of background material about your organization, its mission, and how the program (and your evaluation) relates to the organization's work. People: describe the people who must support the effort and the various groups/people who will participate in the initiative; mention the need(s) that the program is intended to address. Program: a detailed description of the program you will be evaluating and the logic model that presents the theory of change the program supports.
Purpose of the Evaluation	Provides descriptions of the following: Evaluation Purpose: explain why the evaluation is occurring now, what it is intended to determine, and how the results might influence the program. Description of Similar Efforts: describe other evaluations that have been conducted for this program or similar programs, in an effort to optimize your evaluation by being informed by the work of others. Approaches: describe the approaches you intend to use in your program evaluation.

SECTION	DESCRIPTION AND GUIDANCE
Necessary Supporters	Name and discuss the relevance of the evaluation to the person requesting the initiative (e.g., superintendent), the full range of thought partners and supports, and the people who will participate in your initiative.
Contextual Factors	Describe any known risks or other anticipated concerns that could impact doing the evaluation or the results you intend to obtain.
Evaluation Questions	Present your evaluation questions and describe their relevance to stakeholder(s). Evaluation questions can be further defined, if you choose, by using subquestions. Tool 13 Presenting Evaluation Questions provides questions and corresponding subquestion examples.
Methods	Identify the data and the sources for obtaining that data that will be used to answer each evaluation question.
Summary of Data Collection Procedures	Summarize your data collection procedures by identifying each approach and tool you will use to obtain the required data.
Timeline	Present a timeline with milestones to describe the evaluation process.

Three Program Evaluation Models

21

There is no shortage of perspectives on "how" to do program evaluation. Guidance is typically found in what's called an **evaluation model.** You can use these models to scaffold your thinking about your program evaluation—in other words, "what" is measured—and your approach to the program evaluation—"how" it is measured. I've selected three models to share with you because they each lend themselves to the evaluation of education-based initiatives.

Evaluation Model Warning Label

Evaluation models can help guide your program evaluation efforts. But the use of a model should not override the unique context that your initiative—the organization, people, and program—involves. Models should inform not enslave evaluation work. Expert evaluators use models as a basis for an evaluation but often modify the model to accommodate their evaluation needs. An evaluator might even integrate two models to address the wide-ranging outcomes of a more complex initiative.

Evaluation Model 1: The Four Levels

Donald Kirkpatrick (Kirkpatrick & Kirkpatrick, 2006) developed the Four Levels model to evaluate training programs. This model is especially relevant to professional development efforts in districts and schools. Its guidance can be adapted and applied to almost any learning experience. As you review, note how each level provides increasing evidence of initiative accomplishments and outcomes.

Table 21.1   Kirkpatrick's Four Levels of Evaluation

LEVEL	DESCRIPTION	DATA	EXAMPLES
1	**Reaction** How do participants respond to the training?	End-of-class surveys, feedback forms to measure participant satisfaction	Teachers attend a professional development session to learn a new pedagogical approach. They complete a survey following the class.
2	**Learning** Have participants mastered the learning objectives? Do they possess the targeted confidence, attitudes, and commitment?	End-of-class tests of knowledge and skill, surveys to assess confidence with learned skills, designed to measure mastery of stated learning objectives	Teachers participating in training are asked to demonstrate the new pedagogical approach in a mock classroom exercise.
3	**Behavior/ Application** How do participants apply their learnings in the workplace?	Observations, self-assessments, examination of work products (i.e., lesson plans) to measure application of learned skills	Back in the classroom, teachers are observed to assess application of the pedagogy while teaching their students. Teachers might also self-assess their success in applying the new approach.
4	**Results** In what way has the training effort benefitted the organization? What is the return on the training investment?	Mixed methods, leveraging multiple data sources, to make judgments about how the organization's work has improved as a result of the participants' increased performance	Student performance could be used as an indicator of results. You might evaluate the difference in student performance in matched classrooms where teachers applied the new pedagogical approach and classrooms where teachers had not yet implemented the new approach.

I find Kirkpatrick's model especially helpful when working with leaders who have little experience with evaluation. I use it to help them understand the range of ways a program can be evaluated. Often, people's concept of evaluation is limited to end-of-training surveys and similar, less rigorous approaches. Such "Level" 1 data can certainly be useful to an evaluation effort. But by itself, it typically falls short of evaluating the type of program outcomes a learning experience is intended to bring about.

Critics of the Kirkpatrick model have suggested that it lacks the necessary complexity to accommodate the full range of a program's outcomes. Indeed, some have asserted that the model is oversimplified and "does not consider individual or contextual influences in the evaluation of training" (Bates, 2004, p. 342). Others point to the fact this model does not provide for collecting unintended outcomes (meaning, outcomes not predefined by those leading the initiative).

With those limitations acknowledged and the knowledge that evaluation models are meant to inform—not dictate—your evaluation approach, I believe Kirkpatrick's model provides an especially helpful scaffolding that evaluators can use to help project supporters understand an evaluation effort. It offers a similarly helpful organizing structure against which you can define areas to be addressed by most any evaluation effort. For larger efforts where professional development may be one of many program components, the Four Levels of Evaluation can be used to inform evaluation of the training component.

Additional Information About Kirkpatrick's Four Levels of Evaluation

Kirkpatrick website with background information and resources: http://www.kirkpatrickpartners.com/OurPhilosophy/tabid/66/Default.aspx

Additionally, Bates (2004) has offered a critical analysis of the Kirkpatrick model which provides context I find helpful, when I'm using the Four Levels of Evaluation.

Evaluation Model 2: Jacobs' Five-Tiered Approach to Evaluation

Francine Jacobs (Jacobs, 1988) first published the holistic Five-Tiered Approach to Evaluation in 1988 to address the full project or program life cycle. Jacobs believes that any program effort should include evaluation and that evaluation should be part and parcel of the program work from the earliest stage of the project. Ultimately, programs must be prepared to measure outcomes. But the evaluation work should long precede outcomes measurement. It should serve to complement program activities from the very start (defined as "preimplementation" in Jacobs' model).

Table 21.2	Jacobs' Five-Tiered Approach to Evaluation		
TIER	ACTIVITY	DESCRIPTION	EXAMPLES
1	Preimplementation	Occurs during the earliest program planning and involves needs assessment with the targeted participants(s)	Conducting interviews, surveys, or examination of existing sources to determine, prioritize, and/or select the needs to which the program will respond
2	Accountability	Documentation of program progress to participants, leadership, and funding agency	Documenting participation or program use, number of planned program efforts implemented, number of online resources accessed, time on task
3	Program Classification	Formative evaluation where data is used to assess the current program status (what is working, where there is opportunity for improvement) and provide feedback for program improvement and optimization	Program participant surveys, interviews with people who must approve and support the initiative
4	Progress Toward Objectives	Evaluation of short-term outcomes to determine if the outcomes are being achieved as a result of program implementation and use/participation	Relevant indicators of early program impact, such as test scores, lesson plans, and so forth. Short-term outcomes should be defined in evaluation plan and measured at this tier.
5	Program Impact	Overall judgments of program effectiveness—as measured by short- and long-term outcomes	Changes in participant and organizational performance over time. Long-term outcomes should be defined in evaluation plan and measured at this tier.

Jacobs' (2003) offers the following intentions that stand behind her evaluation model:

- It uses a broad and inclusive definition of evaluation, considering needs assessment, implementation study, monitoring activities, and outcome-based accountability all as legitimately within its purview.

- It is incremental, developmental, and systemic in nature, assuming that both the programs themselves and their investments in evaluation will change over time.

- It recognizes a range of purposes for engaging in evaluations, acknowledging different needs at different times in a program's evolution.

- It supports a "many chefs, few diners" orientation to evaluation design, placing program participants at the core of the planning process. (p. 67)

As I have suggested, the Jacobs model takes a *big tent* and *participatory* approach to evaluation. It is big tent because it integrates evaluation into the full program life cycle, which begins with the initial needs assessment work. It is participatory because it guides the evaluator to involve key leaders, initiative supporters, and those who will need to participate in the evaluation—from providing input on planning, through feedback across the program's implementation, and ultimately to measure program outcomes. Whether or not you make use of the Five-Tiered Approach, these two fundamental elements of the model are worthy to achieve in any evaluation effort.

Additional Information About Jacobs' Five-Tiered Approach to Evaluation

Jacobs, F., & Kapuscik, J. (2000). *Making it count: Evaluating family preservation services.* Family Preservation Evaluation Project, Department of Child Development, Tufts University.

An example of the Jacobs model applied to program evaluation can be found here: https://archives.joe.org/joe/2002april/iw1.php

Evaluation Model 3: Stufflebeam's Context, Input, Process, Product (CIPP) Evaluation Model

Stufflebeam (2003) offers the Context, Input, Process, Product (CIPP) Evaluation Model as a "framework for guiding evaluations of programs, projects, personnel, products, institutions, and evaluation systems" (p. 31). Developed in the late 1960s, it was designed to "improve and achieve accountability for U.S. school programs, especially those keyed to improving teaching and learning in urban, inner city school districts." Stufflebeam's beliefs about the purpose of evaluation and his evaluation model are worth noting: "The model's underlying theme is that evaluation's most important purpose is not to prove, but to improve" (p. 31).

As a result, when leaders use the CIPP model, they're pursuing evaluation as a continuous improvement effort.

There are four central elements to Stufflebeam's model:

Context: Examines the context of the program—from formative needs assessment work to summative judgments about whether program goals are present and whether program outcomes were responsive to the identified participant needs.

Input: Here, evaluators assist with program planning formatively by reviewing program plans and processes against targeted goals and outcomes. They may make recommendations for alternative approaches as a result.

Process: Evaluation of the program's implementation formatively and documentation of the full implementation summatively. Note that process documentation is critical to interpreting product evaluation results.

Product: Informs decisions about continuing the program and, ultimately, documents the achieved outcomes and the cause(s) of those results. Note that to determine cause, you need to have clearly documented the process.

It is interesting to note that CIPP is a product of the context in which it was originally developed—one of continuously improving teaching and learning in inner city schools decades ago. Yet it remains highly relevant in today's educational environment. Leaders are constantly challenged to make ongoing decisions about which programs to implement in order to achieve the best possible outcomes. CIPP provides an evaluation framework that is responsive to the participants, the organization, and the program. Figure 21.3 (Stufflebeam, 2003) summarizes the CIPP model, with examples of both formative and summative uses of the model for each of the four components.

Additional Information About Stufflebeam's Context, Input, Process, Product (CIPP) Evaluation Model

Fitzpatrick, J., Sanders, J., & Worthen, B. (2011). *Program evaluation: Alternative approaches and practical guidelines* (4th Ed.). Allyn & Bacon.

Checklist for implementing Context, Input, Process, Product (CIPP) Evaluation: https://www.wmich.edu/sites/default/files/attachments/u350/2014/cippcheck list_mar07.pdf

Table 21.3	Stufflebeam's Context, Input, Process, Product (CIPP) Evaluation Model Components	
COMPONENT	**IMPROVEMENT/FORMATIVE EVALUATION**	**ACCOUNTABILITY/ SUMMATIVE EVALUATION**
Context	Guidance for choosing goals and assigning priorities	Record of goals and priorities and bases for their choice, along with a record of assessed needs, opportunities, and problems
Input	Guidance for choosing a program/service strategy Input for specifying the procedural design, schedule, and budget	Record of the chosen strategy and design and reasons for their choice over other alternatives
Process	Guidance for implementation	Record of the actual process and its costs
Product	Guidance for termination, continuation, modification, or installation	Record of achievements, assessments, compared with needs and costs, and recycling decisions

Stufflebeam, 2003, p. 35

Your "Best" Evaluation Model May Be Your Own

I have briefly reviewed three program evaluation models that are frequently used in educational program evaluation. As you have reviewed these models, you have likely noted some commonalities. For example, the models accommodate both **process measures** and **outcome measures**—in other words, evaluating the work being done (process) and the impact that work has (outcome). You may have also noted that each model includes some judgment of worth to answer a more general question: Were the achieved program outcomes reasonable when considered against the program investments?

Call upon these models whenever you're contemplating an evaluation approach for a given initiative. Make use of multiple models by integrating relevant components to produce an approach that is responsive and "right-sized" to your initiative. By keeping these three models in mind, you will be able to review evaluation opportunities and envision a range of ways your program could be evaluated and then eventually settle on an approach that matches the program and need. That will lead to an evaluation plan that is responsive to the needs of those supporting your effort and reflective of both the program and the window of evaluation opportunity available.

Developing Evaluation Questions 22

One of the most important things you will do as you continue shaping the evaluation is develop **evaluation questions.** These questions will serve as the foundation on which your evaluation work will take place.

What Is an Evaluation Question?

Evaluation questions provide the "big questions" that you'll seek to answer through the evaluation effort. Who you involve in your evaluation work, the instruments you develop or adopt, the strategies you use to collect the data, and the way you report the findings are all influenced by your evaluation questions.

But these evaluation questions fulfill another critical need. Consider the following scenario:

> An evaluator is hired by a school district to conduct an evaluation of some professional development offered to teachers and leaders to increase community involvement across the district's schools. The evaluator diligently sets about the task by creating some helpful professional development surveys. He also creates some record keeping tools to track the number of teachers and leaders trained and the hours of training received. Results from the survey are extremely positive. Teachers and leaders alike appreciate the engagement strategies they were taught. What's more, they say they plan to use them back at their school sites. The evaluator enjoys writing up the largely positive findings and then delivers the report to the district's director of Community Engagement.

A week later, the phone rings. After reading the report, the executive director ponders, "So, did they end up using any of the strategies? And what difference did this make in the quantity and quality of the community's involvement in our schools?"

You might be surprised that such disconnects are all too common in organizations. When it comes to evaluation efforts, there is an effective way to avoid, or at least mitigate, this happening. If you are thinking about using evaluation questions to *calibrate* your evaluation effort, you are on the right track. In addition to logic models, you will want to use evaluation questions to bring everyone involved—from key leaders "above" the initiative to those implementing and participating in the initiative—together. Use an initial draft of evaluation questions to work toward consensus as to what the evaluation effort will set out to answer. Defined evaluation questions also conveniently establish, simply by omission, what questions won't be answered. In that way, they're useful for "right sizing" the evaluation effort by drawing boundaries around what will be evaluated and what won't. In this way, evaluation questions are a great tool for communicating your intent to everyone involved.

What Makes for a "Good" Evaluation Question?

Writing evaluation questions is, to a degree, an art. As with everything evaluation, *what* you're evaluating should drive your evaluation questions. But more generally, evaluation questions should meet some specific criteria. Tool 12 can be used to review draft evaluation questions and consider their suitability to your evaluation effort.

Now, let's take a closer look at each of these criteria and the role they play in good evaluation questions.

TOOL 12: EVALUATION QUESTION CRITERIA	
Purpose	Produce effective evaluation questions.
Task	Use this tool to review your evaluation questions against key criteria.
CRITERIA	**DESCRIPTION**
Specific	Effective evaluation questions state in specific terms what you seek to know.
Measurable	Effective evaluation questions describe something measurable rather than a broad or abstract construct that is difficult or impossible to measure.

CRITERIA	DESCRIPTION
Feasible	Effective evaluation questions describe something that is possible to answer, using the resources available.
Detailed	Effective evaluation questions name the measure(s) you will use to answer the question, where possible.
Worthwhile	Effective evaluation questions seek answers that are of high priority and of utmost value to key leaders and their organization, in terms of program improvement and impact.

Specific

Successful evaluation questions are specific. They describe exactly what question will be answered by avoiding vague references to broad constructs. Consider the following examples.

EXAMPLE	NON-EXAMPLE
Is the Achieve3000 program implemented with fidelity, as measured by time on task, activities completed, and frequency of progress monitoring?	Is Achieve3000 used with fidelity?

This level of specificity helps for each of the reasons I previously described. It helps calibrate the evaluator, initiative leadership, and those upon whose support the initiative relies, not only about what you're measuring but also what the evidence will be. Additionally, when shared with evaluation participants, it positions the evaluation for what it is: a program improvement effort rather than an evaluation of their individual performance. What if you have many fidelity criteria that would make for a very long evaluation question? In those cases, you can simply reference where the criteria can be found in the question (e.g., "as defined in the Achieve3000 Technical Manual's implementation criteria").

Measurable

A complement to the *specific* criteria, successful evaluation questions are measurable. That means the evaluation question seeks an answer that is fully possible to determine.

Remember all that work to define outcomes in the logic model? You diligently framed both outputs and outcomes that were observable and measurable. Success in that endeavor pays dividends at this stage.

Sometimes, however, the fuzzies slip through. When queried about program outcomes, have you heard things like, "This program ignites a passion for U.S. History," or "The professional development should optimize the instruction provided to our students." What, exactly, would "igniting a passion" look like? Certainly, when it comes to doing the evaluation, you couldn't go looking for flames! Similarly, while we're all for optimizing instruction, how will you know it when you see it? As you take up the challenge of determining the extent to which outcomes are achieved, these broad statements of intent become formidable foes.

Before you can evaluate something, it needs to become measurable. Consider the following examples.

EXAMPLE	NON-EXAMPLE
To what extent are participant motivated to engage in making activities—based upon (a) the value they assign to the program and (b) their level of confidence in being successful at completing the projects?	Does the making program inspire participants?

"Inspire" may manifest itself in countless ways. This planning stage of your evaluation work is an excellent time to make things specific and measurable. In this case, when pressed, they pointed toward motivation. Yes, "motivation" can also mean many different things. Note how the successful example has elaborated the construct of motivation using the criteria of value and confidence as indicators of motivation. That, you can measure.

Detailed

While evaluation questions are primarily offered to document what you seek to know about a given program, it is also a good idea to state how things will be measured. Adding this detail helps confirm that you and everyone relying on your evaluation are "on the same page" about what's being measures and how that will happen. It also helps to avoid the kind of disconnect described in the scenario at the beginning of this section.

EXAMPLE	NON-EXAMPLE
Does use of i-Ready for reading instruction for a minimum of two hours each week improve student reading ability as measured by i-Ready progress monitoring scores, Lexile levels, and district benchmark performance (reading component)?	Does use of i-Ready reading instruction improve student reading ability?

Feasible

It almost goes without saying, but your evaluation questions must be possible to answer. Posing an evaluation question that is beyond your supply of time and resources to answer is unreasonable. Plus, it sets an unrealistic expectation for those who must support your initiative in terms of the results they can expect. To be successful here, reflect on the feasibility of each evaluation question you draft and judge the likelihood of whether producing an answer is possible:

- Within the evaluation period
- Through available data or data that is possible to collect
- Given the available resources

Consider the following examples.

EXAMPLE	NON-EXAMPLE
Do participants who visit the science center demonstrate interest in a science-related career following their visit as indicated by (a) questions posed to their teachers or parents; (b) research they chose to conduct; and (c) requests for additional information?	Do students who participate in annual visits to the science center choose science-related careers after college?

Yes—given unlimited time and resources to track participating students, the non-example question may be feasible. But for most program evaluators, the timeframe and the resources required to track participation and career decisions over a decade later would find the non-example question lacking feasibility.

Worthwhile

There is no shortage of interesting questions about your initiative that you could choose to pursue. For those who take a liking to it, your evaluation questions would be limited only by the time available to produce them. But all questions are not equal. It's unlikely you will have the time and resources necessary to pursue a lengthy list of questions.

This is where you need to be carefully attuned to and seek the input from those who you need to support your initiative. Given this limited opportunity for inquiry, what are the priority questions? What questions are most worthwhile to answer for the organization and its program?

While I would like to provide an example and non-example for these criteria, you will quickly find that it is dependent on the organization and context. A leader with a program that is just beginning to be implemented in the classroom may find formative, early feedback from teachers about their initial impressions highly valuable. A district seeking to determine the impact of a long running curriculum initiative may place less value on feedback, in favor of quantitative evidence of implementation and student achievement.

How Much Would You Pay to Answer That Evaluation Question?

What's an evaluator to do when faced with *more* questions than time and budget will support answering? The answer is *prioritize*.

The prioritization effort should be collaborative and include the initiative's supporters and possibly evaluation thought partners.

- One creative way to begin this process is to provide a longish list of the different questions that could be answered through evaluation.

- Next, tell each collaborator they have $100 to spend.

- Ask them to assign a value, between zero and $100, to each question. The values must total $100.00.

Typically, I take all submitted values and establish an average and standard deviation for each question—which is then shared with the group. The average provides an indication of the relative value of each question to the group of collaborators, and the standard deviation provides some indication of consensus among the group.

I have performed this exercise countless times with a wide range of clients. Every time, it proves insightful as an initial step in focusing the evaluation scope and pushing us closer to consensus.

Avoiding the Evaluation Planning Question Pitfall

I have seen and even authored some evaluation questions that didn't do a very good job of framing the evaluation effort. One often encountered shortcoming is the evaluation question that should be asked and answered long *before* the evaluation begins. This kind of evaluation question describes something you need to do first, before you can answer the *true* evaluation questions that follow. Here is an example:

- What measures do we use to judge the effectiveness of our tutoring center program?

This isn't a bad question to answer. In fact, if you are beginning an impact evaluation of an afterschool tutoring program, it is likely a question you *must* answer. But the time to answer it was during the initiative planning and design stages. Likely, this should be documented in the logic model. It is what I call an evaluation *planning* question rather than an evaluation question. By answering this question early on, you inform the development of the corresponding evaluation question. Then, the resulting evaluation question might be something like the following:

> Do participants in the tutoring program for at least three hours a week realize increased achievement over the academic year, as measured by quarterly benchmark tests in reading and mathematics?

In sum, your evaluation questions should be just that—evaluation questions. They should not be questions about how you will conduct the evaluation.

Organizing Your Evaluation Questions

As you develop your questions, it is also helpful to define the various people who have interest in each evaluation question's specific answers. You should also define the "why" behind each evaluation question that's being asked. Remember, given limited time and resources, you must challenge yourself to prioritize the evaluation questions you will pursue.

Tool 13 provides a helpful way to organize this information alongside your evaluation questions. You will also find that this table is a precursor to a similar "methods" table that will be introduced as you develop your evaluation plan.

TOOL 13: PRESENTING EVALUATION QUESTIONS			
Purpose	Present evaluation questions and subquestions and their rationale.		
Task	Use this tool to detail your evaluation questions, alongside the interested people or groups of people (those who will want to learn from the answers your evaluation provides) and the importance of the question to your program. This table will inform a methodology table you will create as part of your evaluation plan.		
EVALUATION QUESTION	**SUBQUESTIONS**	**PEOPLE WITH INTEREST**	**IMPORTANCE OF QUESTION**
Example: How does the Learn & Grow web-based learning tool impact student achievement as measured by state test scores?	1.1 Does student performance change with use of the program? If so, does it improve or regress? 1.2 Does growth vary based on demographic variables (gender, ethnicity, SES)? 1.3 Is there a usage threshold at which achievement occurs?	Principal Teachers using the Learn & Grow product	To determine the product's contribution to student performance in reading
	2.1		
	3.1		

Data Collection Decisions 23

You've worked to understand the program, its implementation, and its intended impact. You've also carefully defined evaluation questions that hold value for the various people who will be consumers of your evaluation. Your next task is to define the evaluation methods you will use to answer those carefully defined evaluation questions.

There are usually many ways to access the information your evaluation requires, and it is equally likely there is no one "right" way to do so. This is where you get to be creative! Let's take a moment to support good decisions as you engage in crafting methods that are responsive to your evaluation questions.

Weighing the Options

As you get experienced with evaluation, you typically become skilled at weighing the benefits and limitations of any given method or approach based on a range of factors that typically include the following:

- Timeline
- Budget
- Quality or anticipated quality of data (from existing sources or to be collected via an evaluator-created instrument)
- Logistical support for data collection (i.e., conducting a survey)
- Ease of access to a given groups of initiative participants
- Likelihood of participation: Will people fulfill the request for data?
- Potential for participants to provide valid, reliable data (e.g., reading ability, language concerns, controversial topics, etc.)
- Import of a participant group's inclusion in the evaluation effort

Many Data Collection Methods

To answer your evaluation questions, you will typically need data from multiple sources, and you'll typically use multiple approaches or methods to get that data. **Triangulation** is the practice of bringing together data collected from multiple sources and varied methods to fully represent the initiative in a complete and accurate way. By employing multiple methods, you set a goal to produce valid, reliable findings that serve a variety of purposes that include documenting program activities and accomplishments, providing judgments of impact and worth, facilitating improvements, and generating knowledge from which future programs can benefit.

As you consider your evaluation questions, think about the different sources of information and how the data they provide could inform your pursuit of answers. Quantitative data is data that can be analyzed statistically and, as such, is numerical. Qualitative data is non-numerical and often examined for patterns. Usually program evaluation involves both types of data.

I find formulating the evaluation methods to be a wonderfully creative aspect of this work. Where possible, I encourage you to find ways to

- Leverage existing data: Try to make use of information that is already being collected, which also reduces the burden of data collection for program participants.

- Use unobtrusive measures: These are measures that do not require the evaluator to be present or to alter the program environment. Look for artifacts that will be produced as a natural result of the program and consider how they might be used as a data touchstone in your evaluation.

Tool 14 is designed to support your efforts to match methods to your evaluation questions. It summarizes the likely data collection tools found in an evaluator's data collection toolbox.

TOOL 14: DATA COLLECTION METHODS FOR PROGRAM EVALUATION	
A LIST OF DATA COLLECTION METHODS TO CONSIDER	
Purpose	Define a range of data collection methods that can be used in program evaluation.
Task	Use this tool to brainstorm and then weigh the benefits and limitations of a range of data collection methods.

METHOD	DESCRIPTION AND GUIDANCE
Questionnaires and Surveys	Used to record participant attributes (i.e., demographics), perspectives, experiences, intentions, beliefs, and more. Surveys can be tricky to design. Not to worry; I'll provide a bonus section to support your survey development.
Interview	A flexible tool that provides for adjustment of questions by the interviewer "on the fly." Helpful for in-depth exploring of constructs and experiences. Provides opportunities for the interviewer to press deeper as necessary.
Focus Group	People sometimes consider a focus group to be the equivalent of a group interview. That is typically not the case. The goal of a focus group is conversation among the participants. A focus group is helpful for exploring an idea or experience, as well as exploring whether consensus can be achieved by the group around a given topic.
Observation	While typically time intensive, sometimes an evaluator simply must "see" his or her program participants in action. Observation can be informal or driven by a preestablished protocol. A formalized observation can be useful for determining the frequency of behaviors, confirming levels of participation, and so forth. Often, multiple observations are necessary to develop an accurate picture of a given phenomenon.
Assessment	Typically used to test the skills or knowledge of participants, confirming mastery of a training program's objectives, for example. Can take the form of a constructed response instrument (i.e., multiple choice test) or an authentic demonstration of applied knowledge or skills (on-the-job performance assessment).
Extant or Archival Data	This is data that already exists in your organization or from another source. It takes many different forms, and excellent sources that could inform an evaluation are often overlooked. Some examples of extant data include the following: • Data generated automatically by technology participants use (e.g., system use, time on task) • Logs or other records already being kept by the organization (e.g., safety data, accidents, pass/fail rates, etc.) • Scores on required assessments (e.g., state or locally required tests, certification exams, performance within a specific course, etc.) • Data generated by other efforts (e.g., existing customer service survey data, etc.) Because this data already exists, it is almost always the least expensive method to employ. For this reason, evaluators should make it a practice to carefully identify all potential extant data that is relevant to a given evaluation need. Extant data is often an ideal complement to the evaluator-constructed instruments a given evaluation requires.

Lining Things Up

A Critical Point in Evaluation Planning

24

I'll bet you've noticed that designing and conducting an evaluation is a **systematic process**. It exists within the larger systematic process of initiative design and implementation and contributes to our goal of producing and leading initiatives that yield predictable outcomes for those who participate.

One strategy that will help you design an evaluation that is well matched to your initiative is the practice of occasionally looking back as you continue to move forward with your evaluation design. At regular intervals, take time to pause and ask yourself the following questions:

Does the current vision or plan for the evaluation

- Match the types of evidence that will satisfy those whose support I need?
- Reflect the program as presented in the logic model?
- Match what are our most important priorities for inquiry?
- Balance both process and outcome inquiry—such that I'm pursuing the association between the initiative's implementation and its outcomes?
- Represent a realistic and feasible plan that will contribute to optimizing the initiative and also demonstrate its worth?

By asking these questions and acting upon the answers that result, you employ a self-correcting process to the evaluation design. This, in turn, keeps the evaluation focused on the program and stated priorities, thus increasing the likelihood of relevant, actionable results. Yes, that familiar reflective practice applies just as much to effective evaluation as it did to your initiative design.

Lining Things Up: Questions, Methods, Participants, and Strategies

Now it's time to take everything you've accomplished to this point and bring it together. In other words, you will specify the *methods* by which your evaluation will operate.

There is good news: If you have carefully developed and documented the elements covered to this point, you have the necessary inputs to effectively determine your methods. Tool 15 will support your work in documenting your evaluation methodology.

TOOL 15: MATCHING EVALUATION QUESTIONS TO DATA SOURCES			
Purpose	Define measures for each evaluation question and subquestion.		
Task	Use this tool to define the data you will collect or access, such that you can answer each of your evaluation questions. This table will serve as the input for one final table where you summarize your data collection effort by each method.		
EVALUATION QUESTION	**INFORMATION REQUIRED TO ANSWER THE QUESTION**	**SOURCE OF INFORMATION**	**DATA COLLECTION METHOD**
Example: How does the Learn & Grow web-based learning tool impact student achievement as measured by state test scores?	Usage data (time on task) from the system Student performance data from the accountability system Student test scores	Teachers using Learn & Grow District Accountability Office	Extant data: Learn & Grow management system (use and performance data) State test scores for current and past four years
	2.1		
	3.1		

With alignment between your evaluation questions and data sources, you can now summarize your data collection methods. Use Tool 16 to develop a complete list of the methods on which your evaluation will rely.

TOOL 16: SUMMARIZING DATA COLLECTION METHODS				
Purpose	Produce a list of procedures you will employ to collect or access the necessary data.			
Task	Use this tool to detail your evaluation questions, alongside the interested people or groups of people (those who will want to learn from the answers your evaluation provides) and the importance of the question to your program. This table will inform a methodology table you will create as part of your evaluation plan.			
PROCEDURE	**QUESTION**	**DATA COLLECTION SCHEDULE**	**RESPONDENTS**	**SAMPLE**
Example: Review of extant data	Q1 (1.1 thru 1.3) Q1 (1.1 thru 1.3)	October 18–22 October 22–24	Teachers District Accountability Office	Obtain (from teachers) Excel spreadsheet of student data: time on task, student performance over time as measured by Learn & Grow Obtain spreadsheet of state test scores, by student, for 2012 through present
Enter each additional method you will employ (e.g., survey, interview, focus groups, testing, logs, etc.)				

Making Findings Persuasive and Actionable

25

You have engaged your supporters and participants. You have the data. Now you may find yourself in the position of having to share your results with your staff, board members, or funders. If you are in this position, it will be worthwhile to take some time and collect your thoughts.

The worth of your evaluation effort will ultimately be judged by how useful it is to your organization. Sadly, I've encountered many situations where the data was amazing but its presentation wasn't palatable to the very people it was intended to inform. I've even been retained to rewrite and represent the admittedly good raw data that was collected. Success comes when you're able to make your results speak and make them actionable.

In this section, I'll highlight some effective strategies for organizing evaluation findings.

Why Evaluation Reporting Is Critical

What if no one reads your evaluation results? Sadly, the chances of that happening are greater than you might expect. Lengthy, dense evaluation reports that lack organization are a challenge to read. Reports that fail to anticipate the reader—what he or she already knows, will want to know, and will act upon—may be set aside after the first few pages are skimmed. Successful evaluators are good communicators. They are adept at taking a large amount of data, synthesizing it, and oftentimes, boiling it down into key messages that inform their clients and provide the basis for action.

Authoring a "usable" evaluation report begins with careful attention to the needs of key leaders in your organization. Of course, that shouldn't be a surprise. You have been attending to those needs from the earliest planning stages of your evaluation work.

Reporting the Findings: Putting the Audience for Your Evaluation Report First

The past few phases of your evaluation work have found you attending to details. You may have built a detailed survey instrument. Or you may have carefully designed an interview protocol that not only posed questions but also anticipated responses by integrating various "probe" questions to dig even deeper. Then, faced with multiple sources of data, you took to the data analysis task and accomplished it with meticulous attention to detail. In sum, the instrument development, data collection, and analysis efforts are evaluation tasks that found you focusing on the details.

It is now time to consider the bigger picture as you transition from the details to begin organizing what you have learned into an informative and actionable report of findings. Take a moment to picture the various people you so carefully described in your evaluation plan. Bring to mind the reasons they should care about your evaluation results. What do they need to learn about your initiative? How can you best demonstrate the initiative's impact using the data you now possess?

Patton (2008), author of *Utilization-Focused Evaluation*, encourages evaluators to carefully consider answers to the following question: How do we know what we think we know? Patton also suggests that an evaluation's worth is largely determined by its utility and actual use.

As you begin to conceptualize the story you will tell, think about how those supporting your initiative will be able to use the findings you provide. Making recommendations that are largely impractical or impossible will be of limited or no use. Likewise, simply presenting endless results of your data analysis will do little in terms of helping your supporters advocate for the initiative's continued work.

Starting With Your Evaluation Questions

Your evaluation questions provide a great place to begin conceptualizing how you'll present your findings. After all, these are the questions you set out to answer through the evaluation effort. Your supporters also approved these questions, and they are expecting your answers and insight. Take a moment to inventory the evidence you have for each question and subquestion. Use the Evaluation Question and Learnings Inventory tool (Tool 17) to organize your thoughts.

TOOL 17: EVALUATION QUESTION AND LEARNINGS INVENTORY		
Purpose	Inventory available evidence.	
Task	Use this tool to list the available evidence you have to answer each of your evaluation questions and subquestions. Briefly summarize your evaluation learnings.	
QUESTION OR SUBQUESTION	**EVIDENCE: DESCRIBE THE DATA AVAILABLE TO ANSWER THE QUESTION**	**LEARNINGS: BRIEFLY DESCRIBE WHAT YOU BELIEVE THE DATA MEANS**
Example: To what extent do teachers perceive value in the New Math curriculum toward helping students achieve?	71% of teachers surveyed indicated they have seen improvement of students' mathematics skills since implementing New Math. 82% of teachers agreed that the curriculum is easy to use in the classroom; 78% indicated that it has improved their abilities to teach mathematics. 88% of teachers indicate that units in the New Math curriculum aligns only partially with the district's pacing guide.	Responses from teachers suggest that the majority see value in using the New Math curriculum. Teachers describing the curriculum's (1) ease of use and (2) perceived increases in the effectiveness of the instruction provided are primary examples that support the teachers' valuing the curriculum. The lack of alignment between the pacing guide and the New Math curriculum sequence could threaten sustained teacher value. The challenge of matching the curriculum to the pacing guide over time may prove frustrating for teachers, who could then reduce or eliminate their use of the curriculum because of conflicting direction.

(Continued)

(Continued)

QUESTION OR SUBQUESTION	EVIDENCE: DESCRIBE THE DATA AVAILABLE TO ANSWER THE QUESTION	LEARNINGS: BRIEFLY DESCRIBE WHAT YOU BELIEVE THE DATA MEANS

Why Not Just Write Up the Results?

You might be wondering whether this intermediary step between data analysis and authoring results is necessary. The answer is, probably not. Still, I believe that taking time to inventory your findings is time well spent. Here's what I believe to be the benefits of this reflective task:

- Determining the extent to which you can answer each evaluation question

- Giving consideration of the full set of results you have collected

- Prompting your thinking about what data will be emphasized in your evaluation report

- Challenging your careful thought about how you will organize your results and make them easily accessible to your readers

Findings: Organizing the Presentation of Your Data

The next decision you must make is how to present your data within the evaluation report or other document you will use to share the results. I typically call this section of an evaluation report "Findings." However, you may also see it termed "Data Analysis." This is where your multiple sets of data, from a range of participants and other interested and involved people, come together.

There are many ways you can organize your findings, and Tool 18 offers four possibilities. Above all, the approach you take should rest on what will be most readily understood and consumed by those whose support you need. Keep that point in mind as you consider your approach.

TOOL 18: ORGANIZING EVALUATION FINDINGS		
IDEAS FOR ORGANIZING FINDINGS		
Purpose	Making your findings accessible to your leaders and supporters.	
Task	Use this tool to review a range of ways to organize your findings	
APPROACH	**DESCRIPTION**	**BENEFITS AND LIMITATIONS**
Evaluation Question	Perhaps the most straightforward approach, here you present each evaluation question and subquestion with the data you have collected in an attempt to answer.	Promotes consistency throughout your report—from the presentation of evaluation questions to the reporting of findings. Can result in presenting the same data multiple times, since a given set of data typically speaks to more than one evaluation question.
Initiative Participants	The findings are enumerated under the participants and initiative supporters from whom they were collected. The findings section presents each group, along with a summary of data received for each.	The people engaged in the day-to-day work of your initiative are, perhaps, the easiest organizing concept for those reading your report to picture. Often, when reporting, you want to highlight similarities and differences between these folks and the data each has provided. By isolating data to a given group, you have limited opportunity to do so.
Data Collection Strategy	The findings are presented by instrument, data collection strategy, or analysis (i.e., extant data analysis). Results from each analysis effort are presented in turn.	This approach may make sense when there is just one data collection strategy employed for each group of participants and initiative supporters and each data collection effort explore a different evaluation question. Typically, initiative supporters—and those whose support you still must garner—are more interested in findings and less interested in the instruments that were used to obtain them.

(Continued)

(Continued)

APPROACH	DESCRIPTION	BENEFITS AND LIMITATIONS
Thematic	This strategy has the evaluator identifying key themes or "big ideas" that come from the data analysis and presenting the corresponding data under each.	Typically, this approach is somewhat similar to presenting your findings by evaluation question. However, instead of using the questions themselves, you use themes in their place. This allows the evaluator to break the evaluation questions into themes that are familiar and of interest to the leaders and supporters. Requires careful setup at the beginning of your findings section so that the reader understands the structure and can anticipate the organization of findings that follow.

Findings Versus Discussion and Recommendations

Evaluation reports typically include recommendations. Remember, one of the main reasons we engage in program evaluation is to continuously improve the initiatives we lead. Therefore, one decision you'll make is where to present your interpretation of the data and your resulting recommendations. Consider two common approaches:

- Typically, more formal presentations follow the organization of a research paper by separating the presentation of data (Findings) from the interpretation (Discussion) and recommendations.

- More informal presentations of evaluation findings may present the data alongside the evaluator's interpretation. With this approach, be very clear delineating data from opinion.

I suggest you make your choice based on the evaluation, leaders, and other supporters who have a significant stake in the initiative and how you anticipate they'll choose to use your results. The careful planning of both program and program evaluation should quickly lead you to a decision about how formal you need the report to be.

Making Results Useful 26

What if you threw a party and no one came? All the preparation and planning, not to mention the resources you drew upon to make your idea a reality, would go to waste. Unfortunately, the same can be said of many evaluation results. Once you've identified what is and isn't working, you want to message in a way that helps the key players adjust their practices where needed. What you don't want is to have your careful analysis shelved, never to be acted upon.

How does an evaluator keep this from happening? Here is our final checklist to guide your work. Tool 19 addresses ways to make your evaluation effort and results useful.

TOOL 19: MAKING RESULTS USEFUL	
Purpose	Provide a range of strategies for delivering evaluation results that support and promote the use of evaluation findings.
Task	Use this tool as a checklist of things to do throughout the evaluation effort, to increase the chances of your final results being both read and acted upon.
STRATEGY	**DESCRIPTION AND GUIDANCE**
Engage Leadership	Provide regular, brief updates to help initiative thought partners and necessary sponsors remain engaged in your work.
	As you collect data, entice with a quote from a participant or an unexpected, preliminary finding.
	Build up an anticipation for and interest in the final results.

(Continued)

(Continued)

STRATEGY	DESCRIPTION AND GUIDANCE
Catch the Attention	Offer an executive summary or "at-a-glance" overview of your findings and impact—for those who don't have time to read the full report.
	Bullet or use a graphic organizer in the executive summary to quickly and vividly display key findings.
	Entice the reader so they press on to subsequent sections of the report and its detail.
Make It Actionable	You will have a unique perspective on the program gained through evaluation that includes understanding how the program operates (think logic model) and the realities of the program's implementation and impact.
	Make sure your recommendations are carefully grounded in this understanding.
	Work from "what is" to "what should be" by connecting recommendations to current activity.
Build on Identified Strengths	No one wants to receive a negative evaluation report. It can be devastating to learn that an initiative isn't living up to the initial expectations. Of course, the first time your supporters learn this fact should not be upon reading the evaluation report. Rather, they should be briefed all along such that surprises are minimized or eliminated.
	When presenting evaluation results, find strongholds to leverage in the pursuit of optimizing a program.
	Build your recommendations on the established and documented strengths.

You will know you've been successful when

- You hear people talking about your results
- You see changes in the program
- Additional questions are raised for future evaluation efforts

Evaluation Is the Yang to Needs Assessment's Yin

I've come to fully appreciate the reciprocal relationship between needs assessment and program evaluation. They actually share many things in common. They rely on similar data collection strategies. They both seek to understand strengths as well as gaps. And they are both intended to inform the actions of people establishing and running programs. Over time, I've come to think of needs assessment as what you do with new challenges and opportunities. But I've also come to think of program evaluation as part evaluation and part needs assessment.

Program evaluation is the perfect time to "check in" on the needs that led to the program in the first place. Are they being positively affected? Have any new needs sprung up since we last inquired? Program evaluation is also the perfect time to review the program's operation and identify any barriers to full implementation. Based on what you find, you'll recommend solutions to those barriers.

In these ways, program evaluation complements the original needs assessment. It bookends the ongoing cycle that moves from needs, to solutions, to confirmation of impact, and back to needs.

I ask my program evaluation clients, each and every time we field a survey or other inquiry, is there anything else you'd like to know? What's on the horizon? In a couple months, what are you going to wish you knew about the current program that will influence your next effort?

In this way, I work to make my evaluations part **perennial needs assessment.** There is never a shortage of challenges to solve and improvements to be made. Take advantage of your program evaluation–fueled opportunities to connect with other leaders, supporters, and those participating in the initiative to press these efforts for all they can provide.

Wrap-Up for Part III

Initiative Impact

I've had the privilege to share Linda and her team's work with you throughout this book. As you reach the final pages, I want to highlight the team's work related to impact—which, naturally, includes evaluation. To do that, I'm going to revisit some of the earlier findings. What I want you to see is that an up-front investment in needs assessment not only guides the initiative's design . . . it also nicely frames the evaluation to the point you're largely evaluating to confirm elimination of the gaps!

Needs Assessment Paying Off

One of the things needs assessment did for Linda was help define the challenge to which her initiative would respond. You'll recall needs assessment headlines about low numbers of families actually engaging with schools and highly disproportionate engagement interactions when groups based on race and socioeconomic status were compared. Families shared their low level of confidence in being able to successfully interact with the educators and leaders in their child's school. In addition, the needs assessment uncovered the fact that a new curriculum, already in place, had "built-in" family connection materials that were going unused. The teachers hadn't been trained on this extension, so it was essentially present and waiting to be activated. Of course, for that to happen, it had to matter. At the time of the needs assessment, there really was no incentive for teachers to engage families—beyond the possible innate desire to do so. Teachers and site leaders were not evaluated on any dimension of family engagement. Additionally, the team found that reaching parents would likely be made possible—at least in part—through community partners. No matter what the schools did, based on what parents said, building the trust and value for engagement for some parents would need to happen through a trusted partner (i.e., faith-based organization). While the needs assessment findings go deeper and wider than my summary, these are the headlines I've shared to help you see a living example of what results.

The initiative then responded to the full litany of needs. It attended to each finding with a solution system that could enter the school district, leverage strengths, and support change, while pressing toward achieving the defined areas of impact set forth in the logic model.

Tracking Progress and Confirming Impact

The team's evaluation plan built directly off the logic model I shared with you. Of course, let's also note that the logic model emerged in direct response to needs assessment data. So when it came time to collect data in an evaluation effort, it naturally closed the loop on the entire initiative effort. It brought the team full circle, as they measured outputs (implementation) and outcomes (change brought about by the initiative).

In fact, the team used modified versions of many of the needs assessment tools—surveys and interviews—to conduct the evaluation. For example, the parent survey became a standard tool for measuring key outcomes over time that included amounts and types of engagement, plus confidence and value levels specific to engaging with their child's school.

Another pretty smart thing the team did involved the action plans. When they produced the action plan template, they used an interactive Google Doc. It included fields where teachers and site leaders could report their family engagement work over time. In this way, the action plan was both a plan and a tracking tool of each educator's work against their plan. The initiative team is able to monitor in real time things like engagement curriculum implementation, family interaction rates, and beyond.

By the way, those action plan dashboards are also available to each site leader. This year, family engagement efforts were integrated into each teacher's annual evaluation, which clearly demonstrated the importance of the initiative. Site leaders used a dashboard for teachers at their schools to monitor the effort, assess results over time, and coach their staff. With metrics at their fingertips, nothing was left to the imagination. Again, as I suggested, what's measured matters. By integrating family engagement into the annual evaluation and investing in this system to support the initiative, Linda and her team increased the "matteringness" of family engagement in measurable ways.

Keeping the Initiative Alive

So what I'll share last about Linda's work might just be the most important thing she's doing—and will continue to do. She is promoting the results of the ongoing evaluation every chance she gets. Each year, she produces a "State of the District: Family Engagement" report that is disseminated to all levels of leaders. Additionally, she condenses that report into a two-pager of highlights that also talks about ongoing changes to the strategies and focus over time. As the program's champion, she carefully promotes the initiative throughout the school year whenever an opportunity arises—or when she causes an opportunity to arise! In sum, she makes the initiative important . . . not only because it is but because it yields positive results that everyone should hear about. In these ways, she reinforces everyone's ongoing contributions to the important work and also ensures the ongoing buy-in and support of the initiative from the districts top-level leaders and board.

Through Linda's experience, I have presented interesting, composite elements of what are relatively small slices of my life experience designing, implementing, fixing, and evaluating programs and initiatives. So here's to Linda for the living illustration of an initiative gone right. I commend her experiences to what you'll take away from our time together. May it offer memories to guide your initiative adventures.

PART III: DISCUSSION QUESTIONS

Use these questions to check your understanding or share your learnings with your initiative team.

1. How do successful initiative leaders use continuous monitoring to improve and heighten an initiative's impact?

2. What benefits does program evaluation bring to initiative leaders?

3. What are some examples of "course correction," and when does it become necessary?

4. What are the components of a successful evaluation question?

5. What considerations should initiative leaders make when choosing how to organize, present, and share evaluation results?

6. How should leaders leverage the reciprocal relationship between program evaluation and needs assessment?

PACING YOUR PROGRAM EVALUATION EFFORT

Similar to my suggestions for needs assessment and initiative design, your time investment is flexible. What matters is that you engage in some evaluation, if for no other reasons than to (a) understand and adjust your effort to optimize results and (b) have some data at the ready to demonstrate value and a return on the investments made in your initiative. So how long should it take to evaluate an initiative?

> Short answer: Program evaluation is usually flexible. As evaluator, the time investment is largely determined by the scope of the evaluation, which you likely have the ability to influence. The evaluation questions you establish will influence time investments.

> Long answer: An evaluation can be launched to understand implementation or outcomes. Most often, it is a combination of the two. There is a line of thought that suggests to be successful, program evaluations need to be comprehensive. The worries, in part, is that when they are not, the available results will not be viewed as rigorous and questions about their reliability then follow. Done well, I believe any amount of evaluation can benefit an initiative. Where you invest your available time should be determined by (a) your interests in terms of program effects; (b) things you wish to monitor and improve over time; and (c) any anticipated or required reporting of program implementation and impact you are asked, in advance, to provide.

Table 26.1 presents some advice about program evaluation work based on the available time you have.

Table 26.1 Pacing Your Program Evaluation Effort	
IF YOU'RE ABLE TO INVEST	**HERE'S WHAT I RECOMMEND YOU DO FOR PROGRAM EVALUATION**
A Few Days	1. Refresh your understanding of the initiative's genesis with a walk through the needs assessment results and then a review of the initiative plan, including logic model

IF YOU'RE ABLE TO INVEST	HERE'S WHAT I RECOMMEND YOU DO FOR PROGRAM EVALUATION
	2. Bring together a thought partner or two to explore program evaluation possibilities and priorities
	3. Using your logic model and a pencil, draw some tentative boundaries around the part or parts of the model you wish to evaluate and contemplate what you will and anything you won't have as a result; contemplate and revise as necessary
	4. Prioritize data you already have, including data you are already collecting as part of running the program; additionally, when planning initiatives, "bake in" data that can both serve the initiative and its participants, as well as support evaluation
	5. Following your identified evaluation focus, use the provided guidance to develop evaluation questions and line them up with evaluation participants and data sources using the Matching Evaluation Questions to Data Sources tool
	6. Plan your evaluation effort, including the timeline, using the Summarizing Data Collection Methods tool; confirm your evaluation is "doable" within the time you have and can invest
	7. Pursue your data collection as planned
	8. Use the Organizing Evaluation Findings to formulate your reporting approach
	9. Summarize and share results while remembering that a two- or four-page summary, with background, will accomplish more than a traditional, detailed evaluation report
A Few Weeks	Use the few-day ideas but also
	1. Engage your initiative team by gaining their input on evaluation priorities and focus
	2. Enlist the support of a professional evaluator as a thought partner to bring fresh eyes to the opportunity and help you determine focus and approach—even if you do the rest of the work yourself
	3. Benefit from framing the evaluation using an existing evaluation model

(Continued)

(Continued)

IF YOU'RE ABLE TO INVEST	HERE'S WHAT I RECOMMEND YOU DO FOR PROGRAM EVALUATION
	4. With more time available, consider expanding your inquiry through the number of evaluation questions you pursue and the range of data you collect
	5. Iteratively build your evaluation plan while checking in with key thought partners and leaders, to reach a focus that will inform all
	6. Regularly reflect on the logic model and the proposed scope of the evaluation: If pursued, will the evaluation provide the data you need to confirm the initiative's implementation and impact?
	7. Consider a collaborative evaluation effort where you engage a professional evaluator to help plan the evaluation, followed by your team collecting the data and then the evaluator doing the analysis and reporting
	8. Consider the range of people who should be informed about your results and then make decisions about the best format or formats for the results to take
A Few Months or More	Use the few-days and few-week ideas but also
	1. Expand the timeframe during which your evaluation is done
	2. Plan the amount of evaluation needed and whether it is best done by the team or an external evaluator
	3. Consider developing a phased evaluation approach where you first pursue early implementation measures and then gradually increase the investment in pursuing outcome measures—this is especially helpful for recently implemented initiatives
	4. Socialize the evaluation plan—especially the evaluation questions—to gain consensus and establish expectations for evaluation results
	5. Invest time to develop a multi-pronged evaluation reporting approach that provides specific results in digestible formats, based on the range of people who need to receive your results

Epilogue

Looking Ahead

The time has come to look ahead . . . beyond the final pages of this book. I'll make this short.

I trust your adventure applying the ideas I have shared has resulted in newfound understandings about initiative design, implementation, and evaluation. Along the way, I hope you gained some new perspectives on things like human performance, motivation, and voice.

This process should be an enlightening pursuit for leader and team member alike. It brings new insight and changes the way we look at needs and initiatives and the way we pursue evaluation inquiry. It also evolves the way we view our organizations and ourselves. These initiatives have a way of reflecting the very people they involve, from those who create to those who partake. I trust you will also come to find a big part of yourself in what you create.

My hope is that you continue to learn through inquiry, grow in initiative design, and that you find the entire process—including evaluation—a creative endeavor that adds value and offers positive impacts—for the people involved in your initiatives and those of you leading the initiatives. In the following appendices, you will find bonus material, including how to craft surveys, planning focus groups, and replicas of all the tools found within the text.

Appendices

Appendix A

Crafting Surveys

Surveys.[1] Every one of us has been asked at some time to complete a survey. Whether getting your car repaired, purchasing a new living room sofa, or encountering someone who is interested in your political views, the frequency with which we face surveys seems to be ever increasing. Add to that the dawn of electronic survey tools, and it is easier than ever to make a survey, solicit responses, and tally the results. The problem is, not all surveys are created equal. While it may be easy to make a survey, creating an effective, useful survey requires careful thought.

Think about the last survey you encountered. Did you jump right in and complete it? Perhaps you started and then dropped out? Or maybe the invitation didn't compel you to even give responding a chance.

When you contemplate everything that must happen for a survey to yield accurate and actionable data, it can be daunting. Consider just some of the escalating prerequisites to realizing effective results from a survey:

- The invitation must sufficiently motivate the potential respondent to open the survey.

- The survey itself must sustain the initial interest to the point of answering the first questions.

---

[1] I acknowledge that in the strictest sense, the correct term would be "questionnaire," since we are primarily discussing characteristics of the form that receives participant responses. However, I've chosen to use the more familiar term, survey, which by definition includes our primary interest, the form, and the gathering, analyzing, and interpreting tasks that follows.

- The questions must be successfully phrased, anticipate common responses, and read as relevant to the respondent.

- The survey must make sense to the respondent. If the survey results in them feeling lost, finding no place to express their true responses, or leaves them questioning whether they're "doing it right," they will drop out or reduce the care with which they provide answers.

- The questions must be phrased in such a way that each respondent interprets them in the same way so that their answers are comparable.

- The survey must sustain the respondent's interest throughout, to the point of completion.

Fortunately, there are effective ways for addressing many of these potential survey pitfalls, and it is critical to attend to these strategies. Once your survey is in the hands of the right person, what happens is fully up to them. If a question is confusing, you do not have the chance to clarify. If they become frustrated and feel like they're not understanding the flow of the survey, you cannot step in to coach and motivate them. Of all the data collection instruments evaluators can employ, surveys require advance planning and thoughtful design.

What Makes for a "Good" Survey

Successful surveys begin with a clear purpose. You shouldn't be collecting data and thus taking valuable time from people if you are not first clear on the questions you seek to answer. When I say "questions" in this context, I am describing the larger evaluation questions you should have defined as an early step in planning your evaluation effort. Further, in that evaluation plan, you should have identified the specific evaluation questions you will target through your survey instrument. Successful surveys don't typically result from opening your web browser, accessing a survey tool, and beginning to write questions. Therefore, the first rule of survey construction is to know the general questions you seek to answer through the survey responses you will receive.

Successful surveys motivate the people who complete them. A good survey draws in the respondent (the person completing the survey), engages that individual in the program evaluation effort, and compels them to provide a careful, complete response. A second rule for survey design is to provide a survey invitation and introduction that interests the prospective respondent and garners his or her support in your evaluation.

Successful surveys keep respondents engaged as they complete the survey form. Attention to the following survey elements is necessary:

- Deliberate organization or "chunking" of topics covered in the survey

- Short, text-based transitions from one section of the survey to the next

- Clear questions that make sense to the respondent and that are easy to understand

- A reasonable number of survey questions, which are reflective of the overarching evaluation questions you seek to answer and the time and attention span of your respondents

Successful surveys provide accurate, valid, and reliable data. This means that items are carefully constructed, reviewed, and revised as necessary to accurately capture the responses of the people you're surveying. Survey questions and corresponding scales must be viewed the same way by each and every respondent; if respondents interpret questions or rating scales in different ways, you won't be able to compare their responses—since each was rating with different assumptions.

Beginning With a Clear Purpose

The most important consideration, as you begin considering surveying, is knowing what you want to learn from the survey data you receive. Which of your evaluation questions do you seek to answer, at least in part, through surveying? Of course, any given evaluation question may require multiple data collection strategies. However, at this early point in the process, take the time to think about the people who will complete your survey and the information they can provide.

- Why will they want to contribute?
- What benefit might they receive by participating?
- How would you describe their necessary time investment to complete a survey? Are they busy? Can the survey be administered and overseen in a group setting, or are you counting on them to choose to participate on their own time?

- What do you anticipate will be their most significant interests and concerns with the program you are evaluating?

- What is the most important information they can provide to inform your evaluation effort?

A Word About Leading With Surveying

As you consider the different methods you will use to collect data, it is important to assess whether you know enough about the program to construct a reliable survey. Surveys are great tools—but not always. The benefits of surveying include the chance to have respondents classify themselves, their experience or opinions, in a closed-ended fashion.

You are likely familiar with open-ended questions. Here is an example:

- What do you find to be the benefits of reading with your child?

A survey constructed of entirely open-ended questions will take considerable time for the evaluator to review, code, and summarize. In fact, evaluations are often better served by an interview approach to data collection rather than surveys, when our questions are open ended. Interviews provide the chance not only to ask these questions but ask follow-up questions to clarify answers. That's something a survey typically cannot do.

Surveys are a great tool to use when you know enough about your program evaluation participants such that you can construct an instrument that anticipates and accommodates the range of responses they are likely to provide. If you cannot anticipate and accommodate a large percentage of these responses, you are likely not ready to conduct a survey. In this case, you may wish to conduct some interviews and continue "getting smart" about the program you're evaluating before proceeding with survey design. The advantage of surveying in program evaluation is to collect data from many people, to identify trends, and to summarize perspectives in an efficient way.

To summarize this point: If you do not know enough about the program and the perspectives of the participants such that you can (a) ask the right questions and (b) create the right checkboxes to accommodate 80% to 90% of their intended responses, then it's probably best to consider another data collection method or learn more about the program before creating your survey. Certainly, you can always include an "other" category on any item and then receive a limited number of open-ended responses you didn't anticipate. But overall, using a survey means you can successfully predict the range of responses and are providing a quick way for respondents to share their experience, perspectives, and voice.

Motivating Your Prospective Respondents

Think for a moment about all the different times you have been approached, of late, to complete a survey. Now, try to remember the ones you completed. You might also recall surveys you started and then stopped because you became frustrated. In today's fast-paced electronic world, we are readily able to express our ideas in any number of ways. Surveys present just one means of sharing our perspectives. As the person fielding the survey, you want to engage potential respondents and compel them to begin your survey. When they receive an email invitation, you want them to immediately choose to click the "Begin Survey" link and persist until the survey is complete.

Invitations and Introductions

This whole chain of surveying begins by getting the prospective respondent to click the "Begin Survey" button or to put pen to paper if completing a hard copy instrument. For that to happen, you must give careful and deliberate thought to what will motivate people to participate.

Consider the following survey invitation:

> *Hello. I created this survey that I'd like you to complete.*
>
> *Thanks in advance.*

This type of invitation does little to motivate someone's response. Earlier, in the "Beginning with a Clear Purpose" step, I encouraged you to consider what benefits your participants might receive through participation. How will you use the data? How will it help them? Briefly tell them—but be careful about making promises you can't keep. This is a great time to apply what you determined in answer to these questions.

Next, carefully construct an invitation and survey introduction that provides the necessary information so that they will want to respond. This means careful selection of the words you choose, as well as how you organize them on the page. Make things easy to read and the key points stand out by using bulleted lists, boldface text, or other conventions while maintaining a professional look. What follows is one successful example:

Welcome—and thank you for your interest in our program. Our primary goal is to give teachers a voice in the education conversations taking place in communities across the country.

This survey is an important part of that process. It will help set the agenda for your upcoming Town Hall—a conversation we hope you will attend. And it will help public broadcasters in your local community and across the country share your ideas and solutions.

We share a common goal:

To help students achieve and graduate ready for career and college.

Together, we can make positive change that benefits students nationwide.

This survey will take about 20 minutes to complete. Please consider each question carefully and select the response that best matches your experience or perspective. If you prefer not to answer a question, just skip it and move to the next.

Your participation starts today! *While this survey is not short, we hope you will take the necessary time to contribute. We will build our televised program from your responses to this survey.*

Here is another example of a good survey introduction.

Imagine Learning Survey

Welcome!

Educational success for English learners can hinge on their ability to speak, listen, read, and write in English. We are asking you to complete a survey that will help the Anytown School District (ASD) in its implementation of Imagine Learning, so that the students of Anytown can achieve even greater success in school and in their lives.

This survey should take approximately 15 minutes to complete. Please consider each question carefully and select the response that best matches your experience.

Your responses are valuable to gaining an understanding of how Imagine Learning is implemented in the classrooms of the district. This understanding will inform district leadership in their continued support for Imagine Learning's implementation. The evaluation findings will be shared with all respondents in staff meetings later this year.

By clicking continue, you are indicating your consent to be a participant in this evaluation. Your responses are anonymous; your identity will not be recorded nor used in any reporting of results. If you do not wish to answer a question, simply skip that item. If you have questions about this evaluation, please contact . . .

Key things you will want your invitation to include are the following:

- Who is doing the evaluation
- Why the evaluation is being done
- What you intend to gain through the evaluation results
- Why the potential respondent should participate
- What investment a respondent will have to make (approximate time that will be required)
- Any incentives that will be offered in exchange for participation
- How the evaluation results will be used
- A consent statement, identifying the evaluator and who to contact with questions

Note that your invitation and the survey introduction will likely be very similar. I strongly suggest, however, that you take the time to craft an invitation that isn't merely a cut and paste of the survey introduction. Simply repeating the same thing twice will not come across as carefully planned to the person doing the reading. Likely, your invitation should stress the "why" behind responding. While these two components may share some of the same information, the survey invitation should be pithy and stress the benefits realized by participating. The survey introduction will contain all necessary information and a consent statement.

Keeping Respondents Engaged

Your prospective respondent has clicked the "Begin Survey" button and, as a result, transformed into a true respondent. The next challenge is keeping her or him engaged. We have all dropped out of surveys mid-response. As the survey's creator, your goal is to keep that from happening. The good news is that some attention to your survey's design will help ensure those who start the survey remain engaged until they reach the end.

Here are some strategies and corresponding questions to ask yourself as you design your survey to keep your respondents engaged.

Format: Are the questions, where applicable, standardized? This means they follow a similar format and organization, such that the respondent can focus on answering questions rather than interpreting varying question formats. In sum, is the instrument user-friendly and logical.

Chunking: Is the instrument segmented into logical "chunks?" Think through the key "buckets" of information you will fill through the survey responses. Then, chunk your survey into three to five areas. Surveys often begin with a section that is "About You," where respondents provide demographic information. Next, the survey might ask questions about their "Use of the Reading Program," with questions that define how much and what components of the program they have used. It might then move into a "Program Utility" section that finds them assessing how useful the program was in their experience. This should provide some idea of what I mean by "chunking" the survey.

Transitions: You also must provide guidance to your respondents, as they move from one section or chunk to the next. Just like you should write an essay with careful transitions, so too should you provide transitions from one section of a survey to the next. Guide and engage your respondents with helpful, supporting text along the way. Introduce each section, occasionally thank them for continuing and participating. Make these transitions short, conversational, and motivating.

Writing, grammar, punctuation, and mechanics: Is the instrument well written and free of errors? Is the instrument written at a level and with language that reflects the population it targets? Make your survey reflect your targeted respondents by referring to things they know and language that is familiar to them. Let them know this survey was made specifically for them.

Achieving Accurate, Valid, and Reliable Data

Each of the things I have covered in this section is an important element of your survey effort. Without your careful attention, your survey will not garner the support you seek. There is a reason why surveys have notoriously low response rates. The strategies I have shared are designed to support you in countering that trend.

However, no number of responses is going to matter if your questions are not well written, well structured, and capable of returning valid and reliable data. What follows is a checklist of key things to consider when constructing survey items.

Common interpretation: Will each item be interpreted in the same way by your respondents? Make sure to "calibrate" respondents by making the language in your survey clear. Define unfamiliar terms. Name each point on a Likert scale rather than simply numbering them. When each person views any given survey question, you want them thinking identically about what they are rating and the range of ratings that can be assigned. When successful, this means the only thing left to vary is your respondents actual rating or response—the one they assign. That is exactly what you want and what enables you to summarize and compare the data you receive.

Single-barreled questions only: Beware of questions that ask someone to rate two things with a single rating. You will know this question when you see it: "To what extent do you agree that the curriculum is easy and effective to use?" If someone strongly disagrees, does that mean the curriculum isn't easy to use, isn't effective to use, or not easy nor effective to use?

Carefully construct series: When you're requiring respondents to select one particular item in a series, you must make sure these items are mutually exclusive. For example, you would not do the following:

Please indicate how many years have you been teaching.

a. 0–1

b. 2–5

c. 6–10

d. 10–20

e. 20+

This is because someone who has taught for 10 years falls into both option c and d. Likewise, someone with 20 years of experience may interpret both d and e. Thus, you want to make sure all categories are unique. For content where people truly can fall into more than one category, consider using the "Select all that apply" style question.

Avoid ranking questions: While this may simply be my bias, the use of ranking questions can produce very incomplete results. If I ask you to rank three things, this assumes that the distance between things 1, 2, and 3 are all equal. Let's talk ice cream: chocolate, vanilla, and strawberry. For me, I'd rank vanilla, strawberry, then chocolate. But truthfully, I'd never eat chocolate. So, vanilla and strawberry are about the same to me . . . chocolate doesn't even come close. Ranking questions hides this variance that is very real to your respondents. It is typically better to have someone rate each item and then calculate a mean or average rating score. That way, you can still put things in a greatest to least order, but you also know the distance between the ratings.

Standardize question conventions: As you write questions, follow a standard format. For example, your Likert scales should run from low to high across the page . . . or high to low. Avoid changing the direction mid-survey. Remember that your respondent will begin to "learn" your survey from the very first question. He or she will begin to anticipate the items. Changing the formatting and general conventions of your survey midway through may not be noticed by the respondent. Therefore, be consistent, and if you must change some element mid-survey, carefully call your respondent's attention to such changes.

Use open-ended questions judiciously: Remember that open-ended questions will require significant amounts of time to analyze and summarize. Use them only when necessary. If your entire survey is open ended, you likely should be using interviews or focus groups rather than surveys.

Attention to these key design components will help you produce surveys that not only get responses but also produce accurate and useful data. Next time you're asked to complete a survey, take advantage of the opportunity to review how others construct these data collection tools. You can learn quite a bit about what to do and what not to do through the act of taking surveys yourself.

Appendix B

Planning Interviews and Focus Groups

Interviews and focus groups offer two helpful approaches to gaining the insight of various people involved in your program. From those running the program to the program's participants, these methods are useful for giving them the voice they need to share their experiences, learnings, accomplishments, and recommendations. Whether conducting formative or summative evaluations or investigating implementation fidelity or short- and long-term outcomes, it is likely that either *could* be of service to your evaluation effort.

Let's look into what each type of effort involves and requires.

Interviews Versus Focus Groups

Before we go too far, it is important to differentiate between interviews and focus groups. Some actually reference focus groups as focus group interviews. In my evaluation work, I look at these two approaches quite differently.

I've shared before that interviews are of highest value when I lack significant insight about the situation. I frame the typical interview with a list of questions, to which the interviewee responds in real time. Like focus groups, I can adjust the interview questioning as I go. Because that is something you cannot do with other methods like surveys, interviews naturally lend themselves to situations when you cannot fully plan for the range of answers you're likely to encounter. While interviews are usually conducted with a single person, there are times you might do a true group interview. Again, when you think interview, think question followed by answer.

Focus groups are typically different. While interviews follow a question-and-answer format, focus groups are intended to get participants talking. For this data collection method, I'll typically bring together 7–10 individuals for the discussion. The focus group protocol is designed to get folks engaged in back-and-forth dialog. The facilitator's role is to pose topics through carefully designed questions or scenarios and to ensure that robust dialog results. Facilitators should also make sure each participant has the chance to engage. Focus groups are helpful when you want to hear a range of perspectives on a key topic or set of topics. They are also useful if you're interested in investigating the extent to which there is consensus on a given topic. They offer the benefit of not only hearing people's perspectives, but also of hearing how participants receive and react to one another's ideas and shared experiences.

When I use focus groups for evaluation, it is often for purposes of clarifying and extending aggregated results from a survey that preceded the focus group session. I bring together a group of folks who are engaged in the initiative to help me interpret the aggregated results from an earlier survey.

Planning Interviews and Focus Groups

Both interviews and focus groups require careful planning. This includes attention to the following tasks:

- Carefully defining the participant profile you seek to engage in your data collection effort, based on demographics, program role, and level of program engagement.

- Accessing and gaining the commitment to participate from a balanced, targeted sample of individuals that match your intended profile.

- Developing a conversational and complete protocol that includes introductory and consent scripting, followed by questions or discussion topics and any planned follow-ups (often called "probes").

- Ensuring that the resulting protocol is aligned with key evaluation question that you've earmarked for answering through interviews or focus groups.

- Planning how you will document your interaction—where options typically include audio or video recording, or simply notes—and also planning for the transcription or other production of data in preparation for analysis.

- Remaining in frequent contact with those who have agreed to participate so that they remain engaged and committed to the point they choose to attend when the scheduled day and time arrives.

- Determining how you will honor these individuals who make extraordinary contributions to your evaluation efforts (incentives).

These qualitative data collection efforts are neither simple nor straight-forward to execute. When successful, it is typically because they are well-planned and attentive to the participants and their commitments.

Elements of an Interview and Focus Group Protocol

While these two efforts are typically conducted for different reasons, they do share some common elements. While the question strategies may differ, Tool 20 presents some elements that are common to both interview and focus group protocols.

TOOL 20: INTERVIEW AND FOCUS GROUP PROTOCOL ELEMENTS	
Purpose	Define the typical elements found in interview and focus group protocols.
Task	Use this tool to guide development of interview and focus group protocols.
ELEMENT	**DESCRIPTION AND GUIDANCE**
	COMMON ELEMENTS
Introduction	The scripted introduction should set up the session. At a minimum, it should • Thank participants • Explain the goal of the interview or focus group • Describe, in general terms, how the data shared will be used
Consent	Your evaluation may or may not require human subjects oversight. Funded programs do typically require institutional review board involvement. Regardless, you'll want to carefully describe your commitments to those who choose to support your data collection effort. Consider the following where applicable • Request permission to record the session where recording is planned, and explain how the recording will be used by the evaluator

(Continued)

(Continued)

ELEMENT	DESCRIPTION AND GUIDANCE
COMMON ELEMENTS	
	• Make any commitments for anonymity or confidentiality for participant identities and references in the reports you intend to create • Offer participants the option to pass on answering a question or end their session in full, at any time they choose • Give them the chance to have any questions answered, before assenting to participation
Chunking	In the survey section, I covered chunking in some detail. Suffice it to say, chunking should also be used in these protocols. Consider the topics you wish to cover and how they might best be organized and introduced to your participants. Remember to review the time you have available and make sure you've not overdeveloped the protocol with too many sections.
Transitions	Again, as with surveys, transitions are incredibly helpful. I'm often asked to review interview protocols that are presented as a lengthy list of questions. They're neither chunked nor do they offer planned and consistent movement from one question to the next. Suffice it to say, every interview or focus group should be conducted in the same way. I suggest you script the transitions you'll use from one chunk to the next. This will keep your questioning consistent and help to keep your participants focused such that their responses best align with the intent of your questions.
INTERVIEW ELEMENTS	
Question and Answer	As I've described, interviews typically consist of question and answer. Protocols may also include prompts, subordinate to a particular question, that offer the opportunity to deepen inquiry or an alternate question should the first answer be off topic.
Depth	Remember that an interview provides you with the opportunity to explore, in depth, the topics of interest—as defined by your evaluation questions. Your protocol should reflect this. Relative to a focus group, a one-on-one interview offers dedicated time to hear from a single individual in deep and meaningful ways. Likely, your protocol should anticipate the need to probe deeper in the areas you've deemed priority.
Sensitive Topics	Interviews offer an ideal approach for exploring the more sensitive aspects of programs. The one-on-one setting is more conducive to someone opening up as the interviewer gains the trust of the participant. For this reason, your protocol may also seek to include topics that wouldn't be advised in a group setting. These could include judgments about overall program health and operation, as well as personnel-related inquiries.

INTERVIEW ELEMENTS	
Interviewing	Conducting interviews is a bit more forgiving than focus groups. Here, your main responsibility is to gain the trust and cooperation of the interviewee, to the point they are comfortable and forthcoming in answering the questions you pose. You'll also be required to manage the timing such that all of your priority questions are answered within the time your participant has agreed to give. Because you are typically working with a single person, you will find it easier to adjust the protocol and expand and contract when necessary in consideration of time.
FOCUS GROUP ELEMENTS	
Topics and Questions	Focus groups tend to involve presenting topics for participants to discuss. Topics are framed with questions. But instead of posing the question to each focus group participant, the facilitator's job is to promote discussion among participants. The more you can get them talking, the more you stand to learn about their experiences. Focus groups are often initiated to get a reaction to something—a program or a product. As such, they may be a great approach if you seek to evaluate a program to the point of identifying recommended improvements from the participants' points-of-view.
	Your protocol will likely be less detailed, relative to an interview protocol. It should also offer opportunities to expand and contract the discussion so that you're predetermined what should happen when any planned timing goes off track. I typically do this by identifying each prompt's priority, such that I can choose to pose only Level 1 priority prompts should time become short.
Depth	In a focus group, you will not have as much time to hear from each participant. For that reason, the depth at which you explore the involved topics will likely be less, when compared to interviews. In a focus group, you should recognize that you're skimming the surface in favor of quickly getting multiple takes on each topic you cover.
Social Pressure	Know that by its very nature of bringing together a group of people, whether known or unknown to one another, the interaction may be impacted by social pressure. Facilitators must do what they can to make all participants feel at ease and free to share their true feelings and perspectives.
Facilitation	Focus group facilitation is an art. I would argue it requires more skill than conducting an interview simply because you're managing seven to ten or more people's contributions. You'll want to make sure each person has a voice in the discussion. And you'll need to diplomatically redirect the conversation when it veers off track into areas that are of no interest to your evaluation. Finally, timing a focus group can be challenging, especially when you need to balance timing with everyone being heard.
	That said, I personally find it a rewarding challenge to meet. I enjoy bringing out the more quiet and reserved participants while also making myself vulnerable in the spirit of encouraging participants to do the same.

Appendix C

Initiative Design, Implementation, and Evaluation Toolset

	TOOL: 1 REALIZING THE 3VS—VOICE, VIEWPOINTS, AND VISION
Purpose	Develop effective questions to use for planning the evaluation effort with key leaders, thought partners, and potential participants.
Task	Use this tool to brainstorm relevant questions to use when initially working with key leaders and thought partners.
CONSIDERATIONS AND STRATEGIES FOR . . .	
Voice	• Think broadly about *all* of the people who could benefit from your program and make a list. • Reviewing your list, brainstorm ways you can make sure you hear from every type of person and group on the list. • Recognize that people differ in the ways they're willing and able to share their voices. • Consider what would be the ideal means for gaining and amplifying voices of each potential participant profile demographic. • Provide an array of opportunities for intended initiative participants to contribute—from listening sessions, to surveys and interviews, to the means for anonymous input. • Recognize that you, yourself, might not be the ideal person to seek voice from people in each of your potential participant groups—consider whether folks will be open and candid with you or whether you should enlist the support of someone with whom they may be more open.

(Continued)

(Continued)

CONSIDERATIONS AND STRATEGIES FOR . . .	
Viewpoint	• Acknowledge that your own lived experience will differ, perhaps greatly, from that of your future participants.
	• Check your positionality and adopt strategies to keep it in check as you invite input.
	• Dedicate yourself to understanding lived experiences, specific to the needs and the challenge at hand.
	• Ask clarifying questions and pose scenarios and examples to hone your emerging understanding of their viewpoint.
	• Guard against and reject impulses to interpret the viewpoints of others, especially those who differ greatly from yourself, based on your own reality.
	• Assume what you're hearing from an intended participant is fact—because, from their reality, it is exactly that, regardless of contradictory information you may hold.
	• Ask questions and encourage continued sharing to understand the knowledge and beliefs that underlie stated viewpoints.
Vision	• Invite intended participants to create the program by asking what they would do, to share their ideals, their dreams.
	• Use these shared visions to further understand viewpoints by working to understand the interplay between shared viewpoints and visions.
	• Respect any and all visions and ideas shared with you.
	• Resist any statement, action, or body language that could be interpreted as dismissing a shared vision or idea.
	• Assume all shared ideas, including solutions, hold merit.
	• Ask clarifying questions to deepen understanding of both the shared vision and the beliefs that underlie that vision—the what and the why.

TOOL 2: ASKING GOOD QUESTIONS

Purpose	Develop effective questions to use for needs assessment queries with thought partners, supporters, and potential participants.
Task	Use this tool to brainstorm relevant questions for use when initially exploring gaps with thought partners, supporters, and potential participants.

NEEDS

• What led you to select or seek to develop this initiative?

• What do you hope to accomplish through this initiative? In the short term? Ultimately, over time?

NEEDS
• Are there already defined outcomes for this effort? If not, can you describe the outcomes you hope it will achieve?
• What are some of the reasons these types of outcomes aren't already occurring?

PROGRAM OPERATION
• How do you see the initiative being implemented?
• On what timeline should the initiative occur?
• What challenges do you anticipate we might encounter implementing the initiative/using the initiative?
• What are some indicators you use to determine if the initiative is "on track"?

IDEAL RESULTS
• If we could fast forward to a point where the initiative's success was evident, what would we see? How would we know the initiative "worked?"
• What kinds of things would you find helpful to know about the initiative and its impact?
• What types of evidence would you consider persuasive?
• What benefits should participants be able to describe after participating in/using the initiative?
• In what ways will our organization and future efforts look different if this initiative is successful?

TOOL 3: DATA COLLECTION METHODS TO CONSIDER	
Purpose	Define a range of data collection methods that can be used in both needs assessment and program evaluation.
Task	Use this tool to brainstorm and then weigh the benefits and limitations of a range of data collection methods.
METHOD	**DESCRIPTION AND GUIDANCE**
Questionnaires and Surveys	Used to record participant attributes (i.e., demographics), perspectives, experiences, intentions, beliefs, and more. Surveys can be tricky to design such that they receive valid and reliable data that can successfully inform your planning. I share a note about "leading with surveys" following.
Interview	A flexible tool that provides for the adjustment of questions by the interviewer "on the fly." Helpful for in-depth exploring of situations, experiences, and opinions. Provides opportunities for the interviewer to press deeper as necessary.

(Continued)

(Continued)

METHOD	DESCRIPTION AND GUIDANCE
Focus Group	People sometimes consider a focus group to be the equivalent of a group interview. But the goal of a focus group is conversation among the participants. A focus group is helpful for exploring an idea or experience, as well as pressing to see whether consensus can be achieved by the group around a given topic.
Observation	Observation can be informal or driven by a preestablished protocol. A formalized observation can be useful for determining the frequency of behaviors, confirming levels of participation, and so forth. Often, multiple observations are necessary to develop an accurate picture of a given phenomenon.
Assessment	Typically used to test the skills or knowledge of participants, confirming current levels of skill or ability. Can take the form of a constructed response instrument (i.e., multiple choice test) or an authentic demonstration of applied knowledge or skills (on-the-job performance assessment).

TOOL 4: NEEDS ASSESSMENT HEADLINE AUTHORING TOOL	
Purpose	Summarize findings into a finite set of headlines that describes the need in tangible terms.
Task	Use this tool to summarize the key findings of your needs assessment. Think about your team, and others interested in your initiative planning effort, and use language that will be familiar and persuasive to them.
THE GAP	
Primary Gap	Describe the top-level gap—using needs assessment evidence.
Contributing Gaps	Describe other identified gaps that you believe are influencing the primary gap.

BARRIERS AND STRENGTHS

List each headline below, and then describing the barriers and/or strengths that are influencing (causing) the situation.

HEADLINE	CATEGORY	BARRIER/STRENGTH DESCRIPTION
	Skills & Knowledge	
	Value & Confidence	
	Incentives	
	Expectations, Tools & Time	
HEADLINE	**CATEGORY**	**BARRIER/STRENGTH DESCRIPTION**
	Skills & Knowledge	
	Value & Confidence	
	Incentives	
	Expectations, Tools & Time	
HEADLINE	**CATEGORY**	**BARRIER/STRENGTH DESCRIPTION**
	Skills & Knowledge	

(Continued)

(Continued)

HEADLINE	CATEGORY	BARRIER/STRENGTH DESCRIPTION
	Value & Confidence	
	Incentives	
	Expectations, Tools & Time	

HEADLINE	CATEGORY	BARRIER/STRENGTH DESCRIPTION
	Skills & Knowledge	
	Value & Confidence	
	Incentives	
	Expectations, Tools & Time	

HEADLINE	CATEGORY	BARRIER/STRENGTH DESCRIPTION
	Skills & Knowledge	
	Value & Confidence	
	Incentives	
	Expectations, Tools & Time	

TOOL 5: DRAWING CONCLUSIONS FROM YOUR DATA

Purpose	Review both existing and recently collected data in summary form to consider findings, share perspectives on learnings to date, and then explore solutions.
Task	Use this tool to frame the team's review of available data and work toward a shared understanding and tentative solutions.

QUESTIONS ABOUT THE DATA

- Looking across the available data, does it make sense? Is it conceivable this data truly represents the people you need to involve in this initiative?
- What evidence do we have that could confirm these findings accurately reflect the involved people(s) and their experiences?
- Where do the visions and viewpoints of your players come together? Where are they split?
- Is any critical voice or viewpoint not yet represented in our data?
- Is there a specific data point you wish we had that proved impossible to get?

QUESTIONS TO SUPPORT INTERPRETATION

- What are the three biggest takeaways that remain in your minds following your individual reviews of our findings?
- What surprised you most?
- What did you expect to see in the findings that didn't appear?
- Think back to your earliest ideas about this situation—the challenge and the causes. In what ways do these findings differ from your earliest assumptions?

QUESTIONS THAT MOVE TOWARD TENTATIVE SOLUTIONS

- Based on our data, is there evidence a program would offer a positive solution to the primary gap?
- What does the team believe to be the most influential causes? What data supports these conclusions?
- What capabilities are already in place, as part of the system, that stand to support our future efforts?
- What primary and supporting program components will be necessary to positively effect the established causes?
- What do we anticipate will get in the way of the solution or solutions we've discussed? What will we do to reduce the change of that influence?

TOOL 6: SOLUTIONS BASED ON BARRIERS AND STRENGTHS

Purpose	An inventory of examples aligned to each category of causes/capabilities to guide early thinking around a program solution.
Task	Use this tool to review the causes and capabilities you find. Consider example solutions that may address causes; acknowledge examples of strengths that may already be present and leveraged to support your program.

BARRIER/STRENGTH	DEFINITION	POSSIBLE SOLUTIONS/STRENGTHS
Knowledge and Skill	You have the necessary information and sufficient opportunity to practice so that you will be successful	• Professional development and training • Coaching • Reference guides, used during performance • Practice

MOTIVATION	VALUE × CONFIDENCE = MOTIVATION	
Value	How much you care about performing	• Hearing how and why others value performance • Connect performance to real-world application • Connect performance to personal goals and aspirations
Confidence	Your beliefs about whether you will or won't be successful	• Early opportunities for success • Protected opportunities for no- or low-risk practice, with feedback • Seeing the success of others who are perceived to have similar baseline abilities while avoiding comparison of the gap between • "Chunked" application—experiencing mastery of smaller, sequenced tasks that, together, comprise the larger performance • Goal setting and self-tracking of emerging performance to see mastery grow, self-gathering evidence of success
Incentives	Things the organization offers that reward successful performance	• Favorable organizational climate that recognizes and rewards performance • Taking time to notice performance • Balanced feedback and consequences for performance—success and growth-oriented feedback • Monetary or monetized rewards • Further opportunities—for growth, for leadership

ENVIRONMENT	COMPRISED OF TOOLS, EXPECTATIONS, AND TIME	
Tools	Ready access to the tools and resources required for successful performance	• Ready access to necessary technologies and program materials • All resources necessary for performance readily available • Reference guides to guide or enlighten performance while it occurs
Expectations	Clear expectations, sometimes through policy, that align with successful performance	• Directives that prioritize performance • Policy that doesn't contradict performance
Time	Established priority for performance that considers the time commitment necessary and accommodates accordingly	• Set aside time for performance to reasonably occur • Clarity around what time allotment performance will replace, in cases where there is no more time in the day • Integration of efficiencies, to reduce time-to-performance and the time it takes to perform

⬚ TOOL 7: LOGIC MODEL BUILDING TOOL	
Purpose	Produce a logic model to represent the program you will be evaluating.
Task	Use this tool and its guidance to identify inputs, processes, and outcomes for the targeted program. Make sure to ask leadership and the program developer if a logic model already exists.

INPUTS	IMPLEMENTATION		OUTCOMES	
	PROCESSES	OUTPUTS	SHORT-TERM	LONG-TERM/ IMPACT
YOUR PLANNED WORK			YOUR INTENDED RESULTS	
Guidance: Inputs describe the resources that will be directed toward the initiative. You might also think	Processes are the things that will be accomplished to implement the initiative.	Processes lead to outputs. Outputs are metrics by which we can assess the	Short-term outcomes, sometimes referenced as "outputs," typically	Long-term outcomes stem from the goals of the initiative and the needs the

(Continued)

(Continued)

INPUTS	IMPLEMENTATION		OUTCOMES	
	PROCESSES	OUTPUTS	SHORT-TERM	LONG-TERM/ IMPACT
YOUR PLANNED WORK			YOUR INTENDED RESULTS	
about inputs as the "investments" made into the initiative. Consider human, financial, and organizational resources.	Processes describe how the initiative will use the inputs (resources). Consider the intentional program activities, including tools, training, events that, together, are designed to bring about the outcomes.	initiative's implementation progress, including implementation fidelity.	describe accomplishment of the defined processes. Consider what might provide the earliest evidence that the program is having even the most limited impact. Short-term outcomes are typically those things that point to "promising results," which lead to longer-term impact.	initiative was intended to address. These outcomes should describe positive change for the people your initiative will reach. Consider growth in knowledge or skills, positive changes in attitudes or confidence levels (self-efficacy), and desired changes for your participants' actions (performance).

TOOL 8: DEFINING FIDELITY

Purpose	Define the specifics that will be used to determine fidelity of initiative implementation.
Task	Use this tool to discuss and then define each dimension of fidelity for your envisioned initiative.

SECTION	OUR PLAN
Expectations—specific to the content, frequency, duration, and coverage of the initiative's implementation	
Dose—of initiative in which participants are required to engage to benefit (establish dosage boundaries to define successful participation)	
Quality—of initiative implementation (e.g., quality of leadership, program oversight, coaching, teaching, etc.)	
Reactions of People Involved—how we intend to ensure our teachers and students—or whomever the initiative engages—find relevance in their participation	
Initiative Differentiation—how we intend to make certain our initiative is unique and different from others that may address similar outcomes	

TOOL 9: PARTNER READINESS CHECKLIST

Purpose	Guide early review of an opportunity that could benefit from partnership.
Task	Use this tool as a checklist to guide your reflection on your readiness for partnering.

DESCRIPTION AND GUIDANCE

- I believe collaboration can benefit addressing identified needs.
- I have identified and assessed community needs and have chosen to pursue a need that may be better met through collaboration.

(Continued)

(Continued)

DESCRIPTION AND GUIDANCE
• I have realistic expectations about what program-based collaboration will require.
• I am aware of potential partnership challenges, such as overcoming cultural differences and philosophies between our organizations.
• I have identified the contributions our organization can bring to a partnership and the constraints we face and intend to address through a partnership.
• I have identified a shortlist of partners with whom I am comfortable engaging in collaboration.
• I have a basic understanding of the prospective partners' organizations and cultures, and I believe that we can collaborate effectively.
• I feel that my partner's goals are aligned with mine and that our assets complement each other and match the community need.

TOOL 10: INITIATIVE PLAN SCHEMATIC

TYPICAL INITIATIVE PLAN ELEMENTS TO DEFINE AND DOCUMENT

Purpose	Summarize common sections of a successful initiative plan.
Task	Use this tool to guide the development of your initiative plan and the sections it will contain.

SECTION	DESCRIPTION AND GUIDANCE
Introduction	A short and concise overview of the initiative. This section should also name the organization and people involved.
Background	Provides descriptions of the following: Organization: background material about the organization, its mission, and how the initiative relates to the organization's work. People: name those asking for the initiative; briefly describe the full set of people involved as leaders, thought partners, and those who will eventually participate in the initiative.
Needs Assessment Summary	Summarize your needs assessment effort: Outline the different needs assessment tasks you completed. Share the summarized data generated by the needs assessment. Offer your conclusions, based on the summarized data, that justify the initiative you will propose.
Program	A detailed description of the initiative you are proposing: Share and describe the logic model—realizing that many people who read your plan will be unfamiliar with this helpful tool.

SECTION	DESCRIPTION AND GUIDANCE
	Describe the various activities your initiative will involve. Connect them to one another and the initiative-at-large rather than limiting your description to a basic list of bulleted activities. Connect the elements to needs assessment data—such that your reader is readily able to picture how the initiative closely aligns with the needs you've documented.
Timeline	Provide a detailed timeline: Share your commitment for development, including the tasks and the timeline on which they will be completed. Carefully consider sequencing by (a) considering the order in which tasks must be completed—in other words, identifying prerequisite tasks—and (b) identifying tasks that can be pursued in parallel, potentially offering efficiency in your initiative development. Assign members of the initiative development team to each task and then comb the timeline to make sure time expectations are reasonable for each task, as well as each team member's allocation. Offer a sample timeline for the initiative's operation. If it is a program that runs annually, produce a one-year timeline that depicts a typical year.
Roles and Responsibilities	The "who" behind your initiative, make sure to describe the following: The personnel who will be involved in the development. Include descriptions of each role and the amount of time you anticipate each role will require. The personnel required for the initiative's operation. Again, define the roles and time allocations.
Partnerships	If your initiative is relying on services or individuals outside your organization, it is important to describe these partnerships in the plan. Make the role or roles of partners explicitly clear. Also note who on your team will manage the partnership and who will be the point-of-contact for each partnering organization.
Risks and Mitigation Strategies	A successful plan anticipates what could go wrong and has a plan to deal with such "risks" before they even happen. Take some time to brainstorm with your team and define the various barriers you might encounter, the "what ifs" that are on the minds of team members, and any other unwelcome developments that could befall your initiative's success. Then, decide what you would do in each situation. Successful leaders constantly guard against risks and keep them from growing to the point of true threats. Taking some time to anticipate risks at this early juncture will also build your team's collective vigilance as they guard against potential derailments.
Program Monitoring and Evaluation	Later, I'll guide your development of an evaluation plan. At this point, you should spend some time defining how you will monitor the initiative's progress. It is a good idea to also briefly suggest how the logic model-defined outcomes—both short- and long-term—will be measured and when such measurement data will be collected, analyzed, and reported. Once defined, I would also encourage you to circle back to the timeline and add this commitment to monitoring and reporting at the relevant times.

TOOL 11: EVALUATION PLAN SECTIONS

Purpose	Define relevant sections of a successful evaluation plan.
Task	Use this tool to anticipate the information you will cover in your evaluation plan and to begin conceptualizing your evaluation plan document. Moderate the level of detail based on the size of your initiative (school-based versus districtwide and beyond). Think about who might read the plan, and write with the most unfamiliar reader in mind.

SECTION	DESCRIPTION AND GUIDANCE
Introduction	A short and concise overview of the program and need for evaluation. This section should also name the organization.
Program Description	Provides descriptions of the following: Organization: a bit of background material about your organization, its mission, and how the program (and your evaluation) relates to the organization's work. People: describe the people who must support the effort and the various groups/people who will participate in the initiative; mention the need(s) that the program is intended to address. Program: a detailed description of the program you will be evaluating and the logic model that presents the theory of change the program supports.
Purpose of the Evaluation	Provides descriptions of the following: Evaluation Purpose explain why the evaluation is occurring now, what it is intended to determine, and how the results might influence the program. Description of Similar Efforts: describe other evaluations that have been conducted for this program or similar programs, in an effort to optimize your evaluation by being informed by the work of others. Approaches: describe the approaches you intend to use in your program evaluation.
Necessary Supporters	Name and discuss the relevance of the evaluation to the person requesting the initiative (e.g., superintendent), the full range of thought partners and supports, and the people who will participate in your initiative.
Contextual Factors	Describe any known risks or other anticipated concerns that could impact doing the evaluation or the results you intend to obtain.
Evaluation Questions	Present your evaluation questions and describe their relevance to stakeholder(s). Evaluation questions can be further defined, if you choose, by using subquestions. Tool 13 Presenting Evaluation Questions provides questions and corresponding subquestion examples.
Methods	Identify the data and the sources for obtaining that data that will be used to answer each evaluation question.
Summary of Data Collection Procedures	Summarize your data collection procedures by identifying each approach and tool you will use to obtain the required data.
Timeline	Present a timeline with milestones to describe the evaluation process.

TOOL 12: EVALUATION QUESTION CRITERIA

Purpose	Produce effective evaluation questions.
Task	Use this tool to review your evaluation questions against key criteria.

CRITERIA	DESCRIPTION
Specific	Effective evaluation questions state in specific terms what you seek to know.
Measurable	Effective evaluation questions describe something measurable rather than a broad or abstract construct that is difficult or impossible to measure.
Feasible	Effective evaluation questions describe something that is possible to answer, using the resources available.
Detailed	Effective evaluation questions name the measure(s) you will use to answer the question, where possible.
Worthwhile	Effective evaluation questions seek answers that are of high priority and of utmost value to key leaders and their organization, in terms of program improvement and impact.

TOOL 13: PRESENTING EVALUATION QUESTIONS

Purpose	Present evaluation questions and subquestions and their rationale.
Task	Use this tool to detail your evaluation questions, alongside the interested people or groups of people (those who will want to learn from the answers your evaluation provides), and the importance of the question to your program. This table will inform a methodology table you will create as part of your evaluation plan.

EVALUATION QUESTION	SUBQUESTIONS	PEOPLE WITH INTEREST	IMPORTANCE OF QUESTION
1.			
2.			

TOOL 14: DATA COLLECTION METHODS FOR PROGRAM EVALUATION

Purpose	Define a range of data collection methods that can be used in program evaluation.
Task	Use this tool to brainstorm and then weigh the benefits and limitations of a range of data collection methods.

METHOD	DESCRIPTION AND GUIDANCE
Questionnaires and Surveys	Used to record participant attributes (i.e., demographics), perspectives, experiences, intentions, beliefs, and more. Surveys can be tricky to design. See the bonus section on developing surveys for guidance.
Interview	A flexible tool that provides for adjustment of questions by the interviewer "on the fly." Helpful for in-depth exploring of constructs and experiences. Provides opportunities for the interviewer to press deeper as necessary.
Focus Group	People sometimes consider a focus group to be the equivalent of a group interview. That is typically not the case. The goal of a focus group is conversation among the participants. A focus group is helpful for exploring an idea or experience, as well as exploring whether consensus can be achieved by the group around a given topic.
Observation	While typically time intensive, sometimes an evaluator simply must "see" his or her program participants in action. Observation can be informal or driven by a preestablished protocol. A formalized observation can be useful for determining the frequency of behaviors, confirming levels of participation, and so forth. Often, multiple observations are necessary to develop an accurate picture of a given phenomenon.
Assessment	Typically used to test the skills or knowledge of participants, confirming mastery of a training program's objectives, for example. Can take the form of a constructed response instrument (i.e., multiple choice test) or an authentic demonstration of applied knowledge or skills (on-the-job performance assessment).
Extant or Archival Data	This is data that already exists in your organization or from another source. It takes many different forms, and excellent sources that could inform an evaluation are often overlooked. Some examples of extant data include the following: • Data generated automatically by technology participants use (e.g., system use, time on task) • Logs or other records already being kept by the organization (e.g., safety data, accidents, pass/fail rates, etc.) • Scores on required assessments (e.g., state or locally required tests, certification exams, performance within a specific course, etc.) • Data generated by other efforts (e.g., existing customer service survey data, etc.) Because this data already exists, it is almost always the least expensive method to employ. For this reason, evaluators should make it practice to carefully identify any and all potential extant data that is relevant to a given evaluation need. Extant data is often an ideal complement to the evaluator-constructed instruments a given evaluation requires.

TOOL 15: MATCHING EVALUATION QUESTIONS TO DATA SOURCES

Purpose	Define measures for each evaluation question and subquestion.
Task	Use this tool to define the data you will collect or access, such that you can answer each of your evaluation questions. This table will serve as the input for one final table where you summarize your data collection effort by each method.

EVALUATION QUESTION	INFORMATION REQUIRED TO ANSWER THE QUESTION	SOURCE OF INFORMATION	DATA COLLECTION METHOD
1.			
2.			
3.			
4.			
5.			

TOOL 16: SUMMARIZING DATA COLLECTION METHODS

Purpose	Produce a list of procedures you will employ to collect or access the necessary data.
Task	Use this tool to detail your evaluation questions, alongside the interested people or groups of people (those who will want to learn from the answers your evaluation provides), and the importance of the question to your program. This table will inform a methodology table you will create as part of your evaluation plan.

PROCEDURE	QUESTION	DATA COLLECTION SCHEDULE	RESPONDENTS	SAMPLE

TOOL 17: EVALUATION QUESTION AND LEARNINGS INVENTORY

Purpose	Inventory available evidence.
Task	Use this tool to list the available evidence you have to answer each of your evaluation questions and subquestions. Briefly summarize your evaluation learnings.

QUESTION OR SUBQUESTION	EVIDENCE: DESCRIBE THE DATA AVAILABLE TO ANSWER THE QUESTION.	LEARNINGS: BRIEFLY DESCRIBE WHAT YOU BELIEVE THE DATA MEANS.

TOOL 18: ORGANIZING EVALUATION FINDINGS

Purpose	Making your findings accessible to your leaders and supporters.
Task	Use this tool to review a range of ways to organize your findings.

APPROACH	DESCRIPTION	BENEFITS AND LIMITATIONS
Evaluation Question	Perhaps the most straightforward approach, here you present each evaluation question and subquestion with the data you have collected in an attempt to answer.	Promotes consistency throughout your report—from the presentation of evaluation questions to the reporting of findings. Can result in presenting the same data multiple times, since a given set of data typically speaks to more than one evaluation question.

(Continued)

(Continued)

APPROACH	DESCRIPTION	BENEFITS AND LIMITATIONS
Initiative Participants	The findings are enumerated under the participants and initiative supporters from whom they were collected. The findings section presents each group, along with a summary of data received for each.	The people engaged in the day-to-day work of your initiative are, perhaps, the easiest organizing concept for those reading your report to picture. Often, when reporting, you want to highlight similarities and differences between these folks and the data each has provided. By isolating data to a given group, you have limited opportunity to do so.
Data Collection Strategy	The findings are presented by instrument, data collection strategy, or analysis (i.e., extant data analysis). Results from each analysis effort are presented in turn.	This approach may make sense when there is just one data collection strategy employed for each group of participants and initiative supporters and each data collection effort explores a different evaluation question. Typically, initiative supporters—and those whose support you still must garner— are more interested in findings and less interested in the instruments that were used to obtain them.
Thematic	This strategy has the evaluator identifying key themes or "big ideas" that come from the data analysis and presenting the corresponding data under each.	Typically, this approach is somewhat similar to presenting your findings by evaluation question. However, instead of using the questions themselves, you use themes in their place. This allows the evaluator to break the evaluation questions into themes that are familiar and of interest to the leaders and supporters. Requires careful setup at the beginning of your findings section so that the reader understands the structure and can anticipate the organization of findings that follow.

	TOOL 19: MAKING RESULTS USEFUL
Purpose	Provide a range of strategies for delivering evaluation results that support and promote the use of evaluation findings.
Task	Use this tool as a checklist of things to do throughout the evaluation effort, to increase the chances of your final results being both read and acted upon.

STRATEGY	DESCRIPTION AND GUIDANCE
Engage Leadership	Provide regular, brief updates to help initiative thought partners and necessary sponsors remain engaged in your work. As you collect data, entice with a quote from a participant or an unexpected, preliminary finding. Build up an anticipation for and interest in the final results.
Catch the Attention	Offer an executive summary or "at-a-glance" overview of your findings and impact—for those who don't have time to read the full report. Bullet or use a graphic organizer in the executive summary to quickly and vividly display key findings. Entice the reader so they press on to subsequent sections of the report and its detail.
Make It Actionable	You will have a unique perspective on the program gained through evaluation, which includes understanding how the program operates (think logic model) and the realities of the program's implementation and impact. Make sure your recommendations are carefully grounded in this understanding. Work from "what is" to "what should be" by connecting recommendations to current activity.
Build on Identified Strengths	No one wants to receive a negative evaluation report. It can be devastating to learn that an initiative isn't living up to the initial expectations. Of course, the first time your supporters learn this fact should *not* be upon reading the evaluation report. Rather, they should be briefed all along such that surprises are minimized or eliminated. When presenting evaluation results, find strongholds to leverage in the pursuit of optimizing a program. Build your recommendations on the established and documented strengths.

TOOL 20: INTERVIEW AND FOCUS GROUP PROTOCOL ELEMENTS

Purpose	Define the typical elements found in interview and focus group protocols.
Task	Use this tool to guide development of interview and focus group protocols.

ELEMENT	DESCRIPTION AND GUIDANCE
COMMON ELEMENTS	
Introduction	The scripted introduction should set up the session. At a minimum, it should • Thank participants • Explain the goal of the interview or focus group • Describe, in general terms, how the data shared will be used

(Continued)

(Continued)

ELEMENT	DESCRIPTION AND GUIDANCE
COMMON ELEMENTS	
Consent	Your evaluation may or may not require human subjects oversight. Funded programs do typically require institutional review board involvement. Regardless, you'll want to carefully describe your commitments to those who choose to support your data collection effort. Consider the following where applicable: • Request permission to record the session, where recording is planned, and explain how the recording will be used by the evaluator • Make any commitments for anonymity or confidentiality for participant identities and references in the reports you intend to create • Offer participants the option to pass on answering a question or end their session in full, at any time they choose • Give them the chance to have any questions answered, before assenting to participation
Chunking	In the bonus section on survey design, I covered chunking in some detail. Suffice it to say, chunking should also be used in these protocols. Consider the topics you wish to cover and how they might best be organized and introduced to your participants. Remember to review the time you have available and make sure you've not overdeveloped the protocol with too many sections.
Transitions	Again, as with surveys, transitions are incredibly helpful. I'm often asked to review interview protocols that are presented as a lengthy list of questions. They're neither chunked; nor do they offer planned and consistent movement from one question to the next. Suffice it to say, every interview or focus group should be conducted in the same way. I suggest you script the transitions you'll use from one chunk to the next. This will keep your questioning consistent and also help to keep your participants focused such that their responses best align with the intent of your questions.
INTERVIEW ELEMENTS	
Question and Answer	As I've described, interviews typically consist of questions and answers. Protocols may also include prompts, subordinate to a particular question, that offer the opportunity to deepen inquiry or an alternate question should the first answer be off topic.
Depth	Remember that an interview provides you with the opportunity to explore, in depth, the topics of interest—as defined by your evaluation questions. Your protocol should reflect this. Relative to a focus group, a one-on-one interview offers dedicated time to hear from a single individual in deep and meaningful ways. Likely, your protocol should anticipate the need to probe deeper in the areas you've deemed priority.
Sensitive Topics	Interviews offer an ideal approach for exploring the more sensitive aspects of programs. The one-on-one setting is more conducive to someone opening up as the interviewer gains the trust of the participant. For this reason, your protocol may also seek to include topics that wouldn't be advised in a group setting. These could include judgments about overall program health and operation, as well as personnel-related inquiries.

ELEMENT	DESCRIPTION AND GUIDANCE
INTERVIEW ELEMENTS	
Interviewing	Conducting interviews is a bit more forgiving than focus groups. Here, your main responsibility is to gain the trust and cooperation of the interviewee, to the point they are comfortable and forthcoming in answering the questions you pose. You'll also be required to manage the timing such that all of your priority questions are answered within the time your participant has agreed to give. Because you are typically working with a single person, you will find it easier to adjust the protocol and expand and contract when necessary in consideration of time.
FOCUS GROUP ELEMENTS	
Topics and Questions	Focus groups tend to involve presenting topics for participants to discuss. Topics are framed with questions. But instead of posing the question to each focus group participant, the facilitators job is to promote discussion among participants. The more you can get them talking, the more you stand to learn about their experiences. Focus groups are often initiated to get a reaction to something—a program or a product. As such, they may be a great approach if you seek to evaluate a program to the point of identifying recommended improvements from the participants points-of-view.
	Your protocol will likely be less detailed, relative to an interview protocol. It should also offer opportunities to expand and contract the discussion so that you're predetermined what should happen when any planned timing goes off track. I typically do this by identifying each prompt's priority, such that I can choose to pose only Level 1 priority prompts should time become short.
Depth	In a focus group, you will not have as much time to hear from each participant. For that reason, the depth at which you explore the involved topics will likely be less, when compared to interviews. In a focus group, you should recognize that you're skimming the surface in favor of quickly getting multiple takes on each topic you cover.
Social Pressure	Know that by its very nature of bringing together a group of people, whether known or unknown to one another, the interaction may be impacted by social pressure. Facilitators must do what they can to make all participants feel at ease and free to share their true feelings and perspectives.
Facilitation	Focus group facilitation is an art. I would argue it requires more skill than conducting an interview simply because you're managing seven to ten or more people's contributions. You'll want to make sure each person has a voice in the discussion. And you'll need to diplomatically redirect the conversation when it veers off track into areas that are of no interest to your evaluation. Finally, timing a focus group can be challenging, especially when you need to balance timing with everyone being heard.
	That said, I personally find it a rewarding challenge to meet. I enjoy bringing out the more quiet and reserved participants while also making myself vulnerable in the spirit of encouraging participants to do the same.

Glossary

"B-52" model of initiative implementation: the "drive by" model of program implementation; materials are dropped into the school environment with no attention to needs, context, or necessary implementation supports

3Vs voice, viewpoints, and vision: *voice* of people involved in the challenge or opportunity; their *viewpoints* on the current situation; their *vision* for the ideal state and what it will take to reach it

Appreciative inquiry: as applied to needs assessment, inquiry that seeks to understand strengths and possibilities; the opposite of and complement to deficit-based inquiry

Behavioral engineering: an approach to "engineering" success for a given set of participants (teachers, students) that provides them with the necessary skills/knowledge, motivation, incentives, and environmental supports

Champion: individual, typically higher placed in your organization, that supports and promotes the initiative

Confidence: one half of the motivation (expectancy) equation; describes an individual's beliefs about their likelihood of success performing; also referenced as self-efficacy

Continuous monitoring and adjustment: using evaluation results to understand the initiative's implementation and impact and then adjusting as necessary to optimize both elements

Contributing gaps: additional gaps that exist below the primary gap, where there is a difference between current and ideal states; contributing gaps typically need to be solved in order to fully eliminate the primary gap

Countering objectives: the process of advocating for needs assessment and a balanced rather than largely deficit-based approach

Deimplementation: the process of eliminating ineffective practices that, historically, have not produced results

Document review: an analysis of existing materials of all kinds that help you understand the current or ideal states

Early wins: according to Spiro (2012), used to describe successes demonstrating concretely that achieving the change goals is feasible and will result in benefits for those involved

Environment: one-half of the extrinsic barriers to/drivers of performance; the necessary supports—including tools and equipment, expectations, and time—that provide for successful performance

Equitable results: initiative outcomes for all who participate, regardless of demographic differences, entry skills/knowledge/ability

Evaluation model: guidance used to frame the evaluation approach; many evaluation models exist (see Kirkpatrick, for example)

Evaluation plan: document that describes the evaluation effort, including evaluation questions, data collection approaches, and analysis plans

Evaluation questions: broadly designed questions used to guide evaluation

Extant data: data, typically found in documents, that already exists; accessed as part of document review

Fidelity: the extent to which the initiative's implementation matches the plan (e.g., the logic model processes and outputs)

Formative data: in-process data; collected during initiative implementation, to understand the initiative in real-time; complement to summative data

Fresh eyes: setting aside your current understanding, presumptions, and biases and attempting to look at the situation anew

Fuzzies: term coined by Robert Mager to describe broad outcome statements that are inherently unmeasurable; for example, "appreciate democracy"

Gap analysis: the process of defining the difference between the current state and an ideal state

Getting smart: an initial effort to understand the people and the need, the barriers and strengths at play, and what we will accept as successful outcomes

Holistic initiatives: initiatives that have carefully assessed needs, determined barriers and strengths, and then attend to each in the initiative's design

Human/Organization performance categories: barriers to performance and drivers of performance; the four categories are skills/knowledge, motivation value/confidence, incentives, and environment

Incentive: one half of the extrinsic barriers to/drivers of performance; defined as external forces from the organization that influence an individual's performance (reward and recognition, performance simply being noticed)

Initiative plan: the playbook that details the initiative's design, implementation plan, and related details

Intrinsic drivers: barriers/strengths that exist within the individual, composed of skills/knowledge to perform and motivation (value and confidence)

Life dependency test: coined by Robert Mager to test if a skills/knowledge barrier exists; asks, "If their lives depended on it, could they do it?"

Logic model: tool to represent an initiative's design consisting of, at a minimum, inputs, process/outputs, and outcomes

Needs assessment headlines: short sound bytes that summarize needs assessment findings, often used as a call to action

Needs assessment: what we do first to understand current and ideal states while also determining barriers and strengths that impact the challenge presented

Outcome measures: used to measure the initiative's impact; outcomes in the logic model

Outcomes: described in a logic model; measures that are used to evaluate an initiative's accomplishments and impact

Outputs: described in a logic model; measures that can be used to evaluate the initiative's implementation

Perennial needs assessment: the act of ongoing needs assessment; typically accomplished through evaluative thinking

Predictable results: the achievement of defined outcomes through a carefully designed initiative, based on data-defined needs; essentially, the predictable elimination of gaps

Primary gap: typically, the "big" gap, the one that causes a call to action; defined as the difference between the current state of things and some envisioned or defined ideal state

Process measures: used to evaluate the initiative's implementation; outputs in the logic model

Program evaluator: person responsible for understanding and documenting an initiative's impact; typically attends to both the implementation and initiative outcomes

Qualitative: data that is not easily counted nor measured, typically the result of interviews, open-ended survey items, and focus groups

Quantitative: numbers or counts—for example, test scores or ratings on a numbered Likert scale

Root causes: the true barrier or barriers that are allowing a gap to exist; the causes for the gap

Scaling: expanding an initiative's implementation or reach; "scaling it up"

Solution system: the sum total of all the different elements of your initiative that, when implemented together, will allow you to achieve predictable results

Systematic process: step-by-step process, where results of one step are used to inform the next

Thought partners: individuals of all kinds who can help you understand the challenge, plan the initiative, make implementation successful, and share in the initiative's continuous improvement

Three brains: the head brain—in charge of cognition and thinking; the heart brain—regulating emotion; and the gut brain—handling intuition and regulating our sense of self

Triangulation: bringing together data of multiple types and from multiple sources; typically part of program evaluation

Value: one half to the motivation (expectancy) equation; value is intrinsic and describes the importance an individual places on performing (implementing a new teaching pedagogy, scoring high on the state test)

References

Bandura, A. (Ed.). (1995). *Self-efficacy in changing societies.* Cambridge University Press. https://doi .org/10.1017/CBO9780511527692

Barnes, J. V., Altimare, E. L., Farrell, P. A., Brown, R. E., Burnett III, R. C., Gamble, L., & Davis, J. (2009). Creating and sustaining authentic partnerships with community in a systematic model. *Journal of Higher Education Outreach and Engagement, 13*(4), 15–29. http://files.eric.ed.gov/fulltext/EJ905410.pdf

Bates, R. (2004). A critical analysis of evaluation practice: The Kirkpatrick model and the principle of beneficence. *Evaluation and Program Planning, 27,* 341–347.

Brinkerhoff, J. M. (2002). Assessing and improving partnership relationships and outcomes: A proposed framework. *Evaluation and Program Planning, 25*(3), 215–231.

Clarke, J., Dede, C., Ketelhut, D. J., Nelson, B., & Bowman, C. (2006). A design-based research strategy to promote scalability for educational innovations. *Educational Technology, 46*(3), 27–36.

Commonwealth Center for Governance Studies. (2014, November). *Improving community health through hospital: Public health collaboration insights and lessons learned from successful partnerships.* https://uknowledge.uky.edu/cgi/viewcontent.cgi?article=1001&context=hsm_book

Cooperrider, D. L., & Srivastva, S. (1987). Appreciative inquiry in organizational life. In R. Woodman & W. Pasmore (Eds.), *Research in organizational change and development: Volume 1* (pp. 129–169). JAI Press.

Cooperrider, D. L., & Whitney, D. (2001). A positive revolution in change. In D. L. Cooperrider, P. Sorenson, D. Whitney, & T. Yeager (Eds.), *Appreciative inquiry: An emerging direction for organization development* (pp. 9–29). Stipes.

Dean, P. J. (1994). *Performance engineering at work.* International Board of Standards for Training, Performance and Instruction.

DeWitt, P. M. (2022). *De-implementation: Creating the space to focus on what works.* Corwin.

Dusenbury, L., Brannigan, R., Falco, M., & Hansen, W. (2003). A review of research on fidelity of implementation: Implications for drug abuse prevention in school settings. *Health Education Research, 18,* 237–256. https://doi.org/10.1093/her/18.2.237

Education Development Center. (2014). *Partnership effectiveness continuum: A research based tool for use in developing, assessing, and improving partnerships.* https://www.wallacefoundation.org/knowledge-center/Documents/Quality-Measures-Partnership-Effectiveness-Continuum.pdf

Elmore, R. F. (1996). Getting to scale with good educational practice. *Harvard Education Review, 66*(1), 1–26.

Fullan, M. (2007). *The new meaning of educational change* (4th ed.). Teachers College Press.

Gilbert, T. F. (2007). *Human competence: Engineering worthy performance.* Pfeiffer.

Granner, M. L., & Sharpe, P. A. (2004). Evaluating community coalition characteristics and functioning: A summary of measurement tools. *Health Education Research, 19*(5), 514–532. https://doi .org/10.1093/her/cyg056

Hattie, J. (2009). *Visible learning: A synthesis of over 800 meta-analyses relating to achievement.* Routledge.

Jacobs, F. (1988). The five-tiered approach to evaluation: Context and implementation. In H. Weiss & F. Jacobs (Eds.), *Evaluating family programs* (pp. 37–68). Aldine deGruyter.

Jacobs, F. (2003). Child and family program evaluation: Learning to enjoy complexity. *Applied Developmental Science, 7*(2), 62–75.

Kirkpatrick, D. L., & Kirkpatrick, J. D. (2006). *Evaluating training programs: The four levels* (3rd ed.). Berrett-Koehler Publishers.

Lasker, R. D., Weiss, E. S., & Miller, R. (2001). Partnership synergy: A practical framework for studying and strengthening the collaborative advantage. *Milbank Quarterly, 79*(2), 179–205.

Mager, R. F. (1997). *Goal analysis: How to clarify goals so you can actually achieve them* (3rd ed.). CEP Press.

Mager, R. F., & Pipe, P. (1997). *Analyzing performance problems: Or you really outta wanna* (3rd ed.). CEP Press.

Maletz, M. C., & Nohria, N. (2001). Managing in the whitespace. *Harvard Business Review, 79*(1), 102–111.

Marshall, J. (2005). Implementation and web–based learning: The unimplemented program yields few results. *Computers in the Schools, 4*(3), 90–95.

Martin, L. L., Smith, H., & Phillips, W. (2005). Bridging "Town & Gown" through innovative university-community partnerships. *The Innovation Journal: The Public Sector Innovation Journal, 10*(2), 1–16. http://www.innovation.cc/volumes-issues/martin-u-partner4final.pdf

Mihalic, S. (2004). The importance of implementation fidelity. *Emotional & Behavioral Disorders in Youth, 4*, 83–86, 99–105.

Nolan, R. (2011, October 19). *How would you measure the strength of a partnership?* How Matters. http://www.how-matters.org/2011/10/19/measuring-partnership/

Patton, M. Q. (2008). *Utilization-focused evaluation* (4th ed.). SAGE.

Robert Wood Johnson Foundation. (2009, February). *Measuring partnerships in public health.* http://www.hcfo.org/files/hcfo/HCFOfindings0209.pdf

Rossett, A. (2009). *First things fast: A handbook for performance analysis* (2nd ed.). Pfeiffer.

Rummler, G. A., & Brache, A. P. (1996). *Improving performance: Managing the white space in the organization chart.* Jossey-Bass Publishers.

Rummler, G. A., Ramias, A., & Rummler, R. A. (2009). *White space revisited: Creating value through process.* Pfeiffer.

Spiro, J. (2012). Winning strategy: Set benchmarks of early success to build momentum for the long term. *Journal of Staff Development, 33*(2), 10–16.

Stolovitch, H. D., & Keeps, E. J. (1992). *Handbook of human performance technology.* Jossey-Bass.

Stolovitch, H. D., & Maurice, J. G. (1998). Calculating the return on investment in training: A critical analysis and a case study. *Performance Improvement, 37*(8), 9–20.

Stufflebeam, D. L. (2003). The CIPP model for evaluation. In D. L. Stufflebeam & T. Kellaghan, (Eds.), *The international handbook of educational evaluation* (pp. 31–62). Kluwer Academic Publishers.

Vroom, V. (1964). *Work and motivation.* Wiley and Sons.

Wolf, E. R., Krist, A. H., & Schroeder, A. R. (2021). Deimplementation in pediatrics: Past, present, and future. *JAMA Pediatrics, 175*(3), 231–232.

Index

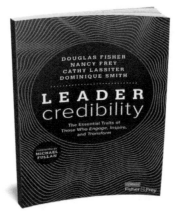

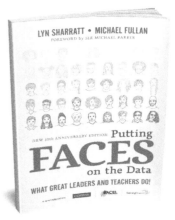

A SAGE Publishing Company

Helping educators make the greatest impact

CORWIN HAS ONE MISSION: to enhance education through intentional professional learning.

We build long-term relationships with our authors, educators, clients, and associations who partner with us to develop and continuously improve the best evidence-based practices that establish and support lifelong learning.